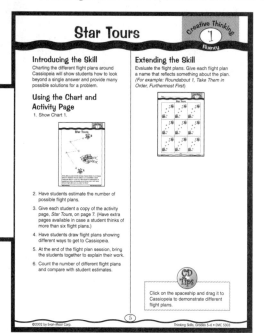

A **teacher page** that provides ideas for introducing the chart, step-by-step instructions for doing the chart activity, and suggestions for extending the skill introduced. Specific hints for interacting with the CD chart are included on this page as well.

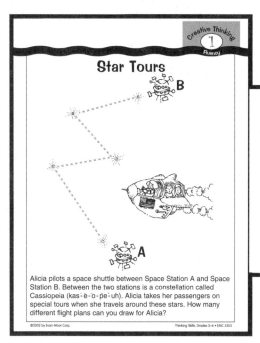

A **chart** that poses a problem or question. Reproduce these charts on overhead transparencies for ease of presentation. Choose the lessons and the order of use that are appropriate to the needs of your students. Note that charts are presented with the simplest skills first, moving to more complex skills.

A reproducible **student page** to be used with the chart or as follow-up practice. Use as many reproducible practice pages as appropriate for your students. These pages may be used with the whole class or as independent practice.

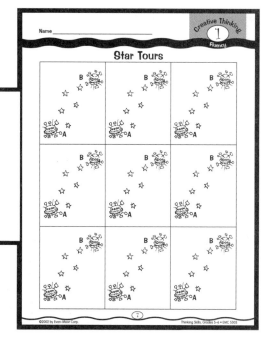

An **Answer Key** for the charts and practice pages begins on page 139.

About the CD-ROM

Loading the Program

1
Put the CD in your CD drive.

This CD-ROM contains both Windows and MacOS programs.

Your computer will recognize the correct program.

2
On some computers, the program will automatically start up. If the program does not start automatically:

Windows—go to My Computer, double click on the CD drive, then double click on Begin.exe.

MacOS—double click on the CD icon on your desktop, then double click on Begin.

3
After the program starts, you will arrive at the main menu.

Main Menu Features

The 44 lessons found in the book are presented in full-color with an interactive element. To present a whole-class lesson, connect your computer to a projection system. As a review, students may be taught to access a specific lesson during their computer time.

 Choose a Topic

1
Click on **Choose a Skill** to display the list of skills.

2
Click on a category. The category will be displayed, along with lesson numbers.

3
Click on a lesson number. The lesson will be displayed, followed by a full-color illustration of a lesson in the book. For example, **Lesson 1, Star Tours.**

4
Refer to the lesson in the workbook. For example, in Lesson 1 you can drag the spaceship to show the different flight plans.

5
After listing and discussing the suggestions from the class, click on **Choose a Lesson** to select the next lesson number, and repeat steps 3 and 4.

6
You may click on **Choose a Skill** to select another category, or click on **Main Menu** and select **Exit** to close the program.

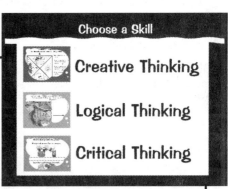

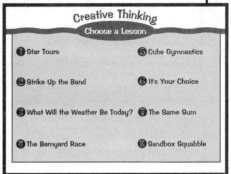

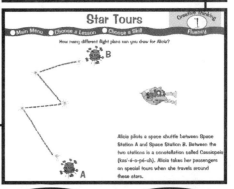

Thinking Skills, Grades 5–6 • EMC 5303

○ View the E-Book

• The charts, practice pages, and answer key are presented in a printable electronic format. You must have Adobe® Acrobat® Reader™ installed to access the e-book. (See installation instructions below.)

Installing Adobe® Acrobat® Reader™

You need to have Acrobat Reader installed on your computer to access the e-book portion of the CD-ROM. If you do not have Acrobat Reader, go to the main menu of the CD and follow these instructions:

1. Place your cursor over the Click Here link. Wait for the hand and then click.
2. When you see the Acrobat Reader Setup Screen, click the "Next" box.
3. When you see the Destination Location Screen, click the "Next" box.
4. When you see the Setup Complete Screen, click "finish."

Your system will now shut down to finish the installation process. Some systems will automatically restart. If yours does not, start it up manually.

• You may scroll through the entire book page by page or open the "Bookmarks" tab for a clickable table of contents.

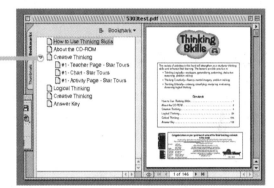

Hint: This symbol, ⊞ for Windows or ▷ for MacOS, means that you can click there to expand the category.

• To print pages from the e-book, click on the printer icon. A print dialog box will open. Enter the page or pages you wish to print in the print range boxes. (At the bottom of the screen, you can see which page of the e-book you are viewing.)

• To exit the e-book, simply "X" out until you return to the main menu.

○ Exit This button closes the program.

Creative Thinking

1 Star Tours

2 Strike Up the Band

3 What Will the Weather Be Today?

4 The Barnyard Race

5 Cube Gymnastics

6 It's Your Choice

7 The Same Sum

8 Sandbox Squabble

Star Tours

Introducing the Skill

Charting the different flight plans around Cassiopeia will show students how to look beyond a single answer and provide many possible solutions for a problem.

Using the Chart and Activity Page

1. Show Chart 1.

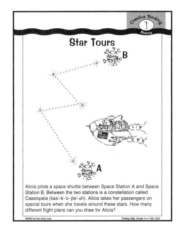

2. Have students estimate the number of possible flight plans.

3. Give each student a copy of the activity page, *Star Tours,* on page 7. (Have extra pages available in case a student thinks of more than six flight plans.)

4. Have students draw flight plans showing different ways to get to Cassiopeia.

5. At the end of the flight plan session, bring the students together to explain their work.

6. Count the number of different flight plans and compare with student estimates.

Extending the Skill

Evaluate the flight plans. Give each flight plan a name that reflects something about the plan. *(For example: Roundabout 1, Take Them in Order, Furthermost First)*

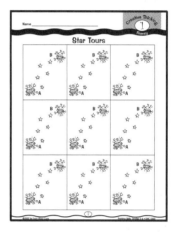

Click on the spaceship and drag it to Cassiopeia to demonstrate different flight plans.

Star Tours

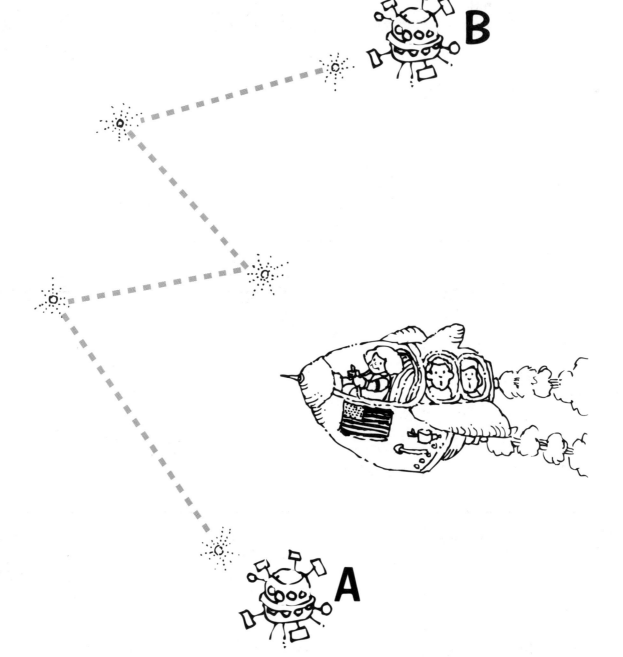

Alicia pilots a space shuttle between Space Station A and Space Station B. Between the two stations is a constellation called Cassiopeia (kas´-ē-ō-pē´-uh). Alicia takes her passengers on special tours when she travels around these stars. How many different flight plans can you draw for Alicia?

Name _____

Star Tours

©2002 by Evan-Moor Corp.

Thinking Skills, Grades 5–6 • EMC 5303

Strike Up the Band!

Introducing the Skill

1. Give six students colored sheets of paper—two red, two white, and two blue.

2. Have students stand in a line at the front of the classroom.

3. Arrange the students so that the colors are in different orders.

4. Record each arrangement on the chalkboard.

   red blue white red blue white

   red red white blue blue white

Using the Chart and Activity Page

1. Show Chart 2.

2. Distribute the activity page, *Strike Up the Band!,* found on page 10. This record page will keep students in step when they are discovering the possible color arrangements for the band. Colors or letters may be used to mark the circles. Some students may need more than one page.

3. Set a goal for the number of arrangements each student should design. Give students time to work on the possibilities.

4. Have students share their work.

5. Discuss the different methods they used to discover the different color arrangements.

Extending the Skill

1. Have students invent a variety of arrangements with different numbers of band members in each row.

2. Developing **fluency** means thinking of many possible answers. Ask students to think of a time when fluency might be important. *(One example: If you know only one way to walk to school and that path is blocked, you wouldn't be able to go to school.)*

Click on the example icon to show one possible color arrangement. Create possible color arrangements by dragging the red, blue, and white circles into the square.

Thinking Skills, Grades 5–6 • EMC 5303

Strike Up the Band!

Get ready for the parade! Alex opened the box with the band's new uniforms. There are four red ones, four white ones, and four blue ones. If the band marches in three rows with four people in each row, how many ways can you find to arrange the colors?

Name _____

Strike Up the Band!

Example:

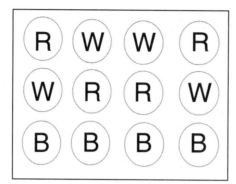

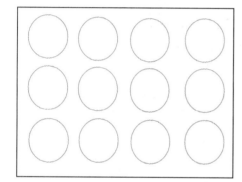   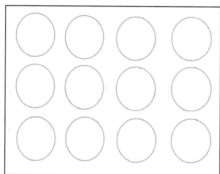   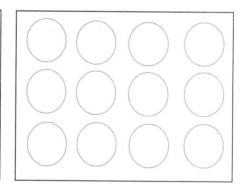

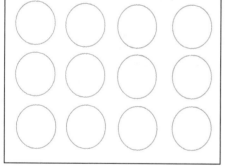   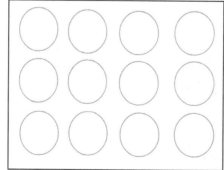   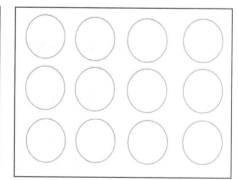

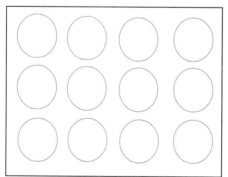   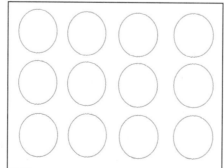

Thinking Skills, Grades 5–6 • EMC 5303

What Will the Weather Be Today?

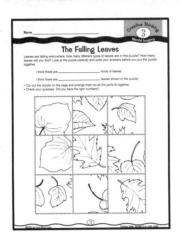

Introducing the Skill

This puzzle will challenge students to think through the problem and visualize the solution.

Using the Chart and Activity Page

1. Have students put pencil and paper away. Tell them that to solve this puzzle they must rely on brainpower.

2. Show Chart 3.

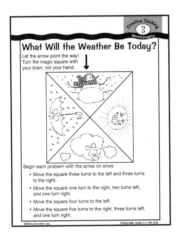

3. Ask students to give the weather prediction after each mental rotation.

4. Check the answer by actually turning the chart.

5. Take time to discuss how various individuals approached the problem.

6. Distribute the activity page, *The Falling Leaves,* found on page 13.

7. Have students predict answers after looking at the puzzle pieces, and then check their answers by cutting the puzzle out and putting it together.

Extending the Skill

1. Choose a picture of an object or a scene. (Student art is fine for this project.)

2. Reproduce the picture, then cut it into nine equal sections like the puzzle on the activity page.

3. Arrange the pieces in a mixed-up square.

4. Ask students to write a description of the original picture.

5. Share the written descriptions and evaluate how accurate they were.

Keyboard students' predictions in the text box. Then click on the turn icons to check predictions.

Thinking Skills, Grades 5–6 • EMC 5303

What Will the Weather Be Today?

Let the arrow point the way!
Turn the magic square with
your brain, not your hand.

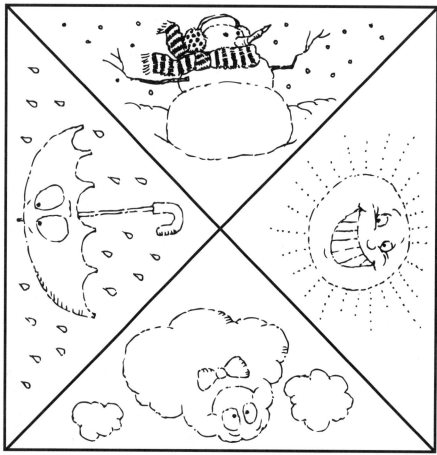

Begin each problem with the arrow on snow.

- Move the square three turns to the left and three turns to the right.

- Move the square one turn to the right, two turns left, and one turn right.

- Move the square four turns to the left.

- Move the square five turns to the right, three turns left, and one turn right.

The Falling Leaves

Leaves are falling everywhere. How many different types of leaves are in this puzzle? How many leaves will you find? Look at the puzzle carefully and write your answers before you put the puzzle together.

I think there are _____ kinds of leaves.

I think there are _____ leaves shown in the puzzle.

- Cut out the blocks on the page and arrange them so all the parts fit together.
- Check your guesses. Did you have the right numbers?

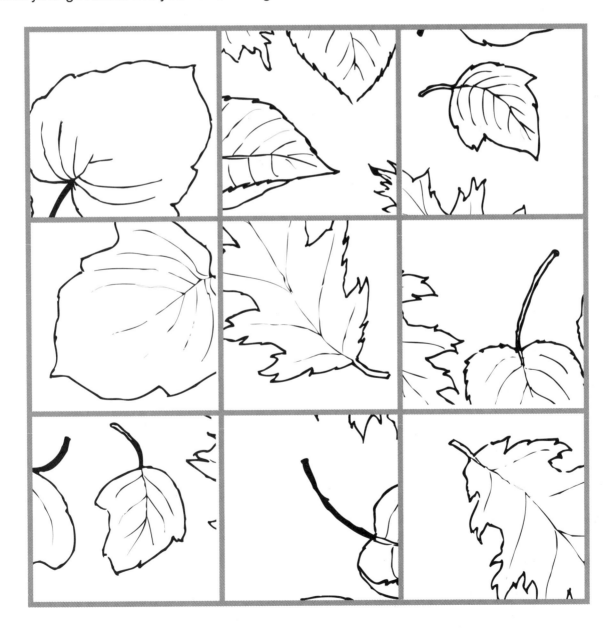

(13)

Thinking Skills, Grades 5–6 • EMC 5303

The Barnyard Race

Introducing the Skill

1. Divide a large square into four triangular sections. Color each section a distinct color.

2. Tape the square to the chalkboard and draw an arrow pointing to one section.

3. Tell students to turn the square with their minds and tell what section the arrow would point to for each of the following:

   one turn left
   one turn right
   two turns left
   two turns left and one turn right

4. Allow students to work mentally and then demonstrate the actual movement.

5. After a number of practice moves, encourage students to share any tricks they developed for keeping track of the mental movements.

Using the Chart and Activity Page

1. Show Chart 4.

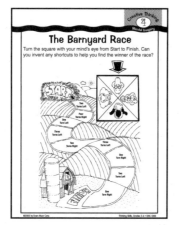

2. Read all the clues to the class slowly. Have students visualize the movements of the square and write down a winner.

3. Go back to the beginning. This time read a clue and, once students predict the arrow's position after the clue, turn the chart to check the predictions.

4. After reading, predicting, and checking each clue, see how many students were correct with their initial predictions.

5. Distribute the activity page, *Who Will Win My Race?*, found on page 16.

6. Students create their own puzzles.

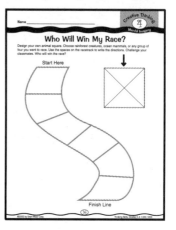

Extending the Skill

Discuss the shortcuts that students discovered as they solved the mental imagery puzzles. They may have found that four turns to the right or left means the square is in the same position. It's possible to solve the puzzles by adding up the turns to the right and to the left, subtracting the smaller number from the larger one, and then mentally moving the square by only the smaller number. For example:
In "The Barnyard Race" there are eleven turns left and eight turns right. Eleven minus eight is three turns. Turn the square three turns left and find the winner—Pig!

Click on the words *left* and *right* to turn the puzzle. Keyboard the name of the winner in the box.

Thinking Skills, Grades 5–6 • EMC 5303

The Barnyard Race

Turn the square with your mind's eye from Start to Finish. Can you invent any shortcuts to help you find the winner of the race?

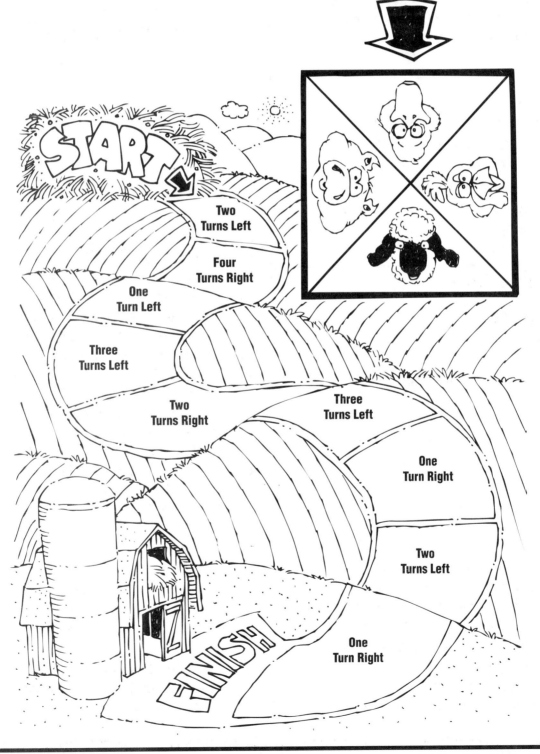

Name _____

Who Will Win My Race?

Design your own animal square. Choose rainforest creatures, ocean mammals, or any group of four you want to race. Use the spaces on the racetrack to write the directions. Challenge your classmates. Who will win the race?

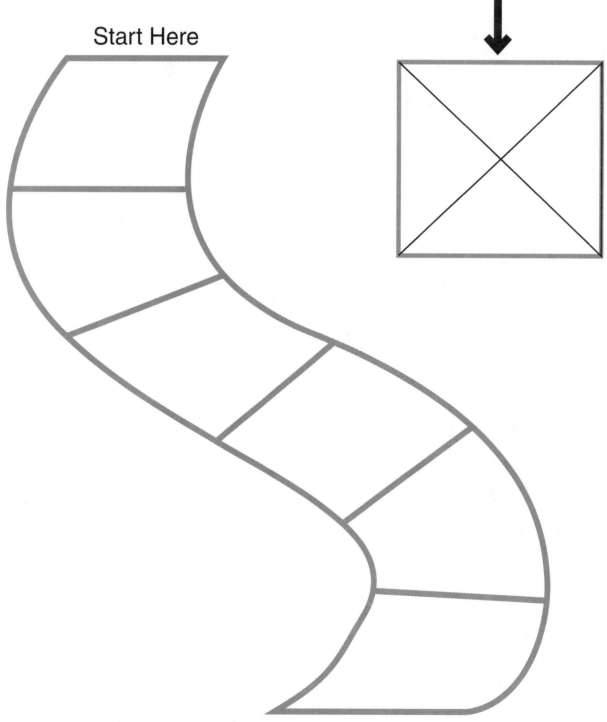

Start Here

Finish Line

16

Cube Gymnastics

Introducing the Skill

1. Have students study dice. They should note the number of dots on each side of the die.

2. Then place the die on a surface and have students predict the number of dots on the side resting on the surface.

3. Turn the die to the right and ask students to give the number of dots again. (Their work with cubes will be easier if they find that the top and bottom sides don't change their location when the cube is rotated to the right or left.)

4. Continue turning the die and ask questions about the relative positions of the dots to help students see patterns. Eventually they will discover that the same number of dots are always opposite each other.

Using the Chart and Activity Page

1. Show Chart 5.

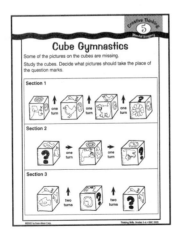

2. Have students predict the answers to each problem on the chart.

3. Prepare a cube with the chart pictures on it. Manipulate the cube to check the answers.

4. Give students the activity sheet, *Where's That Ant?*, on page 19.

5. Help students draw a cube. They may use the cube to record what they know about the position of each picture.

6. Students look at each pictured cube, labeling their blank cube to match the sides they know. After the first three clues, they will know where the ant is located.

7. Then they go back and circle the words to tell the ant's position in each different situation.

Extending the Skill

Students may cover blank or numbered dice with stick-on dots and design their own cube puzzles.

After students have made their predictions, click on the *?* to reveal the correct answer.

Thinking Skills, Grades 5–6 • EMC 5303

Cube Gymnastics

Some of the pictures on the cubes are missing.

Study the cubes. Decide what pictures should take the place of the question marks.

Section 1

one turn one turn one turn

Section 2

one turn one turn

Section 3

two turns two turns

Where's That Ant?

It's picnic time! Fruit, veggies, cheese, bread, and cookies are packed in the picnic box. Watch out! Here come the ants.

Study the sides of the cubes. The ants are on one of the hidden sides: the back, the bottom, or the left side of the cube.

Circle the word that tells where the ants are hiding on each cube.

Back
Bottom
Left

Back
Bottom
Left

Back
Bottom
Left

Back
Bottom
Left

Back
Bottom
Left

Back
Bottom
Left

Thinking Skills, Grades 5–6 • EMC 5303

It's Your Choice

Introducing the Skill

1. Ask students if they have ever made a mistake. Have them tell what kind of a mistake it was. Record different kinds of mistakes on a chart or the chalkboard.

2. Let them know that everyone, even teachers, make mistakes. Some mistakes are easy to correct—a mistake on a math problem is easily erased and recalculated. Deciding what to do about other mistakes can be very difficult.

Using the Chart and Activity Page

1. Show Chart 6.

2. Review the situation on the chart with the class. Discuss their ideas.

3. Distribute the activity page, *What Will You Do?*, found on page 22.

4. Explain that students are being asked to evaluate their own plans and how they relate to other people's plans.

5. Have students write several different scenarios for each problem and then decide which plan is the best.

6. Compare and discuss students' decisions.

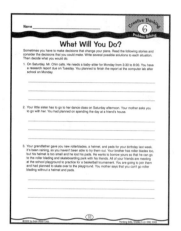

Extending the Skill

Have each student invent a situation similar to the ones on the chart and the student page. Each week present one of these problems and have students write "advice column" solutions.

Click in the text box to keyboard students' responses.

It's Your Choice

What Will You Do?

Sometimes you have to make decisions that change your plans. Read the following stories and consider the decisions that you could make. Write several possible solutions to each situation. Then decide what you would do.

1. On Saturday, Mr. Chin calls. He needs a baby-sitter for Monday from 3:30 to 8:00. You have a research report due on Tuesday. You planned to finish the report at the computer lab after school on Monday.

_____

_____

_____

2. Your little sister has to go to her dance class on Saturday afternoon. Your mother asks you to go with her. You had planned on spending the day at a friend's house.

_____

_____

_____

3. Your grandfather gave you new rollerblades, a helmet, and pads for your birthday last week. It's been raining, so you haven't been able to try them out. Your brother has roller blades too, but his helmet is too small and he lost his pads. He wants to borrow yours so that he can go to the roller blading and skateboarding park with his friends. All of your friends are meeting at the school playground to practice for a basketball tournament. You are going to join them and had planned to skate over to the playground. You mother says that you can't go roller blading without a helmet and pads.

_____

_____

_____

Thinking Skills, Grades 5–6 • EMC 5303

The Same Sum

Introducing the Skill

Solving number puzzles involves the following:

- thinking carefully about the premises of the problem and their implications before beginning

- making careful guesses and then checking them

Using the Chart and Activity Page

1. Show Chart 7.

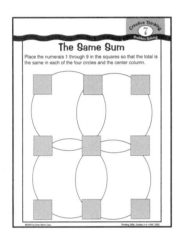

2. Read the directions. Have students restate the premises of the puzzle.

   This puzzle requires that the four numbers in each circle and the three numbers in the center column have the same sum.

   This implies that the numbers in the center column will probably be larger numbers.

3. Write the numerals 1 through 9 on small sticky notes. Place them in the squares and try out possible solutions. Move them around until they are in the correct positions.

4. Distribute the activity page, *Math Puzzlers,* found on page 25.

5. Have students solve the puzzles by using the two strategies demonstrated when the chart puzzle was solved.

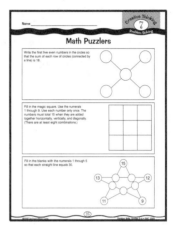

Extending the Skill

Challenge students to create their own number puzzles and magic squares. Create a class puzzle bank or a class puzzle book with the puzzles and answers.

Click in each square and keyboard a number.

Thinking Skills, Grades 5–6 • EMC 5303

The Same Sum

Place the numerals 1 through 9 in the squares so that the total is the same in each of the four circles and the center column.

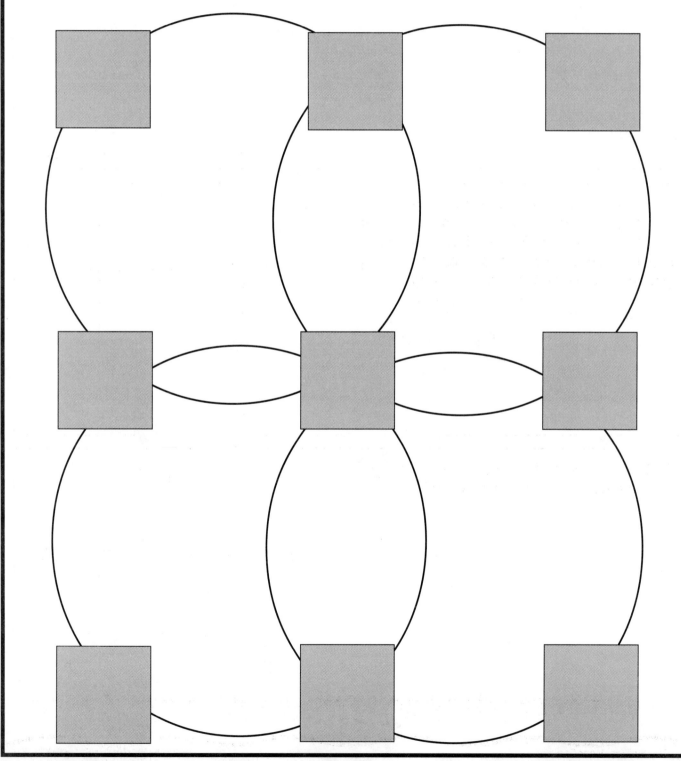

Name _____

Math Puzzlers

Write the first five even numbers in the circles so that the sum of each row of circles (connected by a line) is 18.

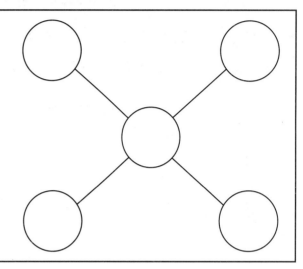

Fill in the magic square. Use the numerals 1 through 9. Use each number only once. The numbers must total 15 when they are added together horizontally, vertically, and diagonally. (There are at least eight combinations.)

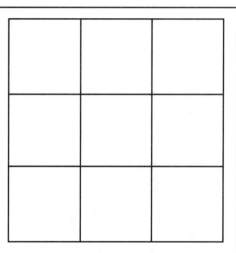

Fill in the blanks with the numerals 1 through 5 so that each straight line equals 30.

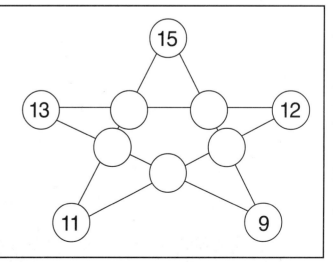

   Thinking Skills, Grades 5–6 • EMC 5303

Sandbox Squabble

Introducing the Skill

1. Give each student a square piece of graph paper with 20 squares.

2. Ask them to divide the square into four equal parts. The parts must be the same size and the same shape.

3. Compare the different divisions students have made. If no student makes an irregular-shaped division, propose one yourself.

Using the Chart and Activity Page

1. Show Chart 8.

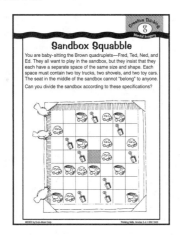

2. Distribute the activity page, *The Sandbox Squabble,* found on page 28.

3. Discuss the problem posed on the chart. Guide students to summarize the important information and list it succinctly on the chalkboard. Students may wish to copy it on their papers.

   Space specifications: *same size*
   same shape
   two trucks
   two shovels
   two cars

4. Discuss possible solutions.

   An immediate tendency is likely to include enclosing space in a square or rectangular shape. A little experimentation should lead the students to conclude that the only way to include the required toys is to use irregular shapes. Add the specification "shape will be irregular."

5. Someone is apt to suggest the idea of figuring out how many squares each boy will get.

   There are 48 squares (not counting the seat), so each boy will get 12 squares. Add the specification "shape will enclose 12 squares."

6. Challenge students to solve the problem. Let students experiment before revealing the solution.

After students have made their divisions, click in the center square of the sandbox to show the correct division.

Thinking Skills, Grades 5–6 • EMC 5303

Sandbox Squabble

You are baby-sitting the Brown quadruplets—Fred, Ted, Ned, and Ed. They all want to play in the sandbox, but they insist that they each have a separate space of the same size and shape. Each space must contain two toy trucks, two shovels, and two toy cars. The seat in the middle of the sandbox cannot "belong" to anyone.

Can you divide the sandbox according to these specifications?

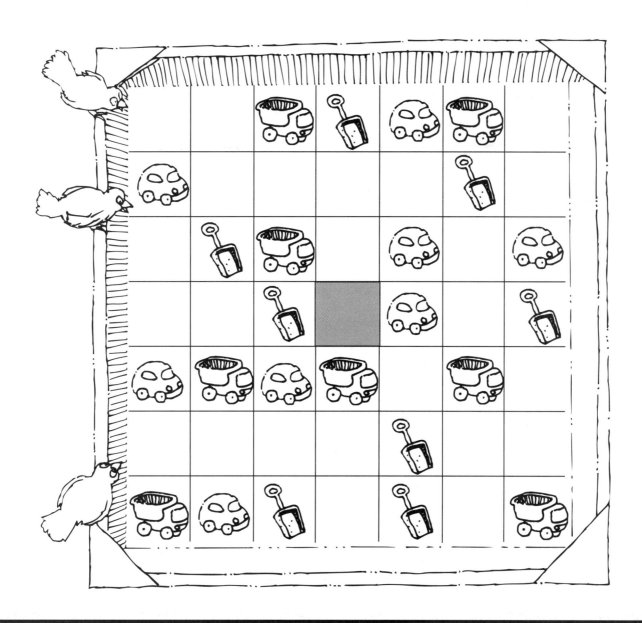

The Sandbox Squabble

Logical Thinking

©2002 by Evan-Moor Corp.

Thinking Skills, Grades 5–6 • EMC 5303

Mirror, Mirror

Introducing the Skill

1. Write the words *delighted, devastated,* and *disappointed* on the chalkboard.

2. Set the scene.
   A handsome prince strode into the royal barbershop. It was time for a haircut. His curly locks were so long that he could not see the target when he practiced his archery. The new barber took one look at the prince and began to cut…

3. Give these clues to help students guess the one descriptive word that tells about how the prince felt when he looked in the mirror.

   • *The word ends with -ed.*

   • *The word has 3 pairs of identical letters.*

   • *The word has 4 vowels.*
   (Answer: devastated)

Using the Chart and Activity Page

1. Show Chart 1.

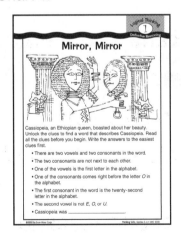

2. Read the clues and discover an adjective that describes Cassiopeia.

3. Give each student the activity page, *Character Clues,* on page 32.

4. Have students solve the example for Puss.

5. Each student should choose a character, write a descriptive word about that character, and then write clues that would help others discover the descriptive word.

6. Share student work.

Extending the Skill

Read the story of Cassiopeia and Perseus to your class. Interesting versions can be found in *Gods and Heroes, Myths and Epics of Ancient Greece* by Gustav Schwab and *D'Aulaire's Book of Greek Myths.*

Click on the blank to keyboard the letters that spell the answer.

30

Mirror, Mirror

Cassiopeia, an Ethiopian queen, boasted about her beauty. Unlock the clues to find a word that describes Cassiopeia. Read all the clues before you begin. Write the answers to the easiest clues first.

- There are two vowels and two consonants in the word.

- The two consonants are not next to each other.

- One of the vowels is the first letter in the alphabet.

- One of the consonants comes right before the letter *O* in the alphabet.

- The first consonant in the word is the twenty-second letter in the alphabet.

- The second vowel is not *E, O,* or *U.*

- Cassiopeia was _____.

Character Clues

With a group of your classmates, brainstorm a list of interesting characters you have read about in fairy tales and stories. Write one word that tells about each character. For example, the queen in the story "Snow White" was jealous of Snow White's beauty.

Choose one of the characters. Write clues for the letters in the word that describe the character. Ask other students to follow the clues and write the word that describes your character.

Here is an example to get you started.

Puss, in the story "Puss in Boots", is a _____ cat.

- The missing word has two vowels.

- Both vowels are the same.

- One vowel in the word is the fifth letter in the alphabet.

- The last letter comes before *S* in the alphabet.

- The first two letters are the same consonants that blend together in the word *clue*.

- The fourth letter in the word is written with two straight lines.

- The fourth letter is not *T, L, Y,* or *X*.

Strange Travelers

Introducing the Skill

Explain to the class that a chart can provide a method of recording the information given so that you arrive at correct answers through a process of eliminating incorrect answers. Sometimes you must read through all the clues before recording any information.

Using the Chart and Activity Page

1. Show Chart 2.

2. Read the following introductory information.

   The seven passengers on Alicia's space shuttle come from different planets. Their eating habits make them uneasy seatmates. When the passengers buy tickets, Alicia gives them special seat numbers so everyone has a calm trip, even at mealtime. Help Alicia give out seat numbers for the passengers. One passenger must sit in the skydome to watch for comets and asteroids.

3. Ask students to survey the picture and everything written on the chart before they make a seating arrangement.

4. As a class, read the clues and make seat assignments. Be sure to explain the reasoning behind each seat assignment.

5. Challenge students to apply the deductive reasoning skills that they have gained by completing the student activity page, *Who's New at the Zoo?,* on page 35.

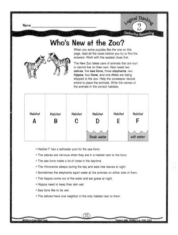

Extending the Skill

Ask students to think of a time when they have had to gather information and eliminate incorrect answers in order to determine the correct answer. (This can be an important test-taking strategy.)

Click and drag the passenger names to the correct seat on the space shuttle.

Strange Travelers

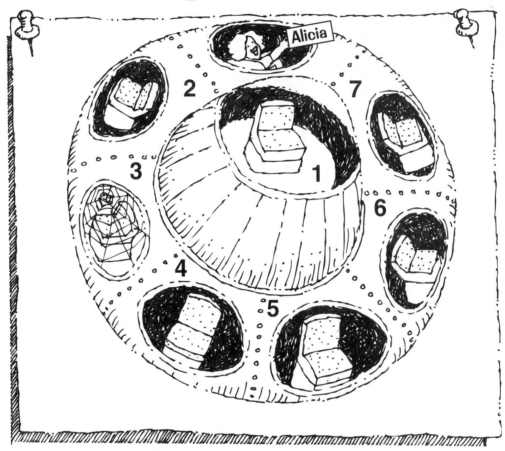

Alicia

Seat Assignment Clues

- Spider likes to eat flies.

- Bird likes to eat flies and spiders.

- Rabbit likes to eat carrots.

- Human won't sit by an insect-eater.

- Human can sit next to Rabbit because Human is a vegetarian.

- Fly annoys his neighbors because he buzzes and crawls over them looking for food.

- Guinea Pig is a messy eater who loves carrots. If she sits next to Bird, Bird pecks up her mess.

- Bird only sits next to one other passenger.

PASSENGER LIST

Spider

Carrot

Bird

Rabbit

Human

Fly

Guinea Pig

Name _____

Who's New at the Zoo?

When you solve puzzles like the one on this page, read all the clues before you try to find the answers. Work with the easiest clues first.

The New Zoo takes care of animals that are hurt or cannot live on their own. Next week two **zebras**, five **sea lions**, three **elephants**, two **hippos**, four **lions**, and one **rhino** are being shipped to the zoo. Help the zookeeper decide where to place the animals. Write the names of the animals in the correct habitats.

Habitat A	Habitat B	Habitat C	Habitat D fresh water	Habitat E	Habitat F salt water

- Habitat F has a saltwater pool for the sea lions.
- The zebras are nervous when they are in a habitat next to the lions.
- The sea lions make a lot of noise in the daytime.
- The rhinoceros sleeps during the day and eats tree leaves at night.
- Sometimes the elephants squirt water at the animals on either side of them.
- The hippos come out of the water and eat grass at night.
- Hippos need to keep their skin wet.
- Sea lions like to be wet.
- The zebras have one neighbor in the only habitat next to them.

Thinking Skills, Grades 5–6 • EMC 5303

Analogies

Introducing the Skill

1. If your students are not familiar with analogies, write the following simple analogy on the chalkboard:

   Sock is to foot as glove is to hand.

2. Explain that an analogy examines the relationship between two pairs of items. *(A sock is a covering for a foot; a glove is a covering for a hand.)*

3. Tell students that when they are working with analogies, they need to look for the similarity or connection between the two items. Then they can find other items with the same connections.

Using the Chart and Activity Page

1. Show Chart 3.

2. Ask students to determine the connection between a pair of scissors and a barber. *(The scissors are used by the barber in his line of work, which is cutting hair.)*

3. Then ask students how that connection can be applied to the second part of the analogy. *(The missing word must be someone who uses a tractor in his/her line of work—a farmer.)*

4. Students complete the activity page, *Analogies,* found on page 38.

5. Share student work by having them tell the relationship they used to form the correct analogies.

Extending the Skill

Have each student write one analogy. The two sets of words used must be related in the same way.

Many types of relationships can be used to form analogies, for example:

place—bear : den :: bee : hive

numerical—5 : 10 :: 3 : 6

opposites—hot : cold :: day : night

object-to-action—ear : hear :: bed : sleep

object-to-purpose—food : eat :: bed : sleep

part-to-whole—runner : sled :: wheel : wagon

sequence or degree—minute : small ::
gigantic : big

Drag the correct word onto the line to complete the analogy correctly.

Analogies

Scissors are to a **barber** as

a **tractor** is to a _____.

Finish the analogy with one of these choices:

doctor   **wheel**   **farmer**   **field**   **crop**

Name _____

Analogies

Read each analogy. Think about the relationship between the first two items. Choose the word that will make the second part of the analogy have the same relationship.

1. A **sheet** is to a **bed** as a **rug** is to the _____.

    carpet   cover   floor

2. A **laptop** is to a **computer** as a **watch** is to a _____.

    clock   machine   time

3. A **horse** is to a **herd** as a **bird** is to a _____.

    den   nest   flock

4. A **piano** is to a **trumpet** as **broccoli** is to _____.

    vegetable   cabbage   garden

5. A **squirrel** is to **squirrels** as a **mouse** is to _____.

    nest   mouses   mice

6. **Pizza** is to **Italy** as **tacos** are to _____.

    burritos   Mexico   Canada

7. **Quiet** is to **loud** as **heavy** is to _____.

    light   big   ton

8. **Still** is to **calm** as **small** is to _____.

    tall   big   little

Thinking Skills, Grades 5–6 • EMC 5303

More Analogies

Introducing the Skill

Complete Chart 4 as an introduction to the analogies.

Using the Chart and Activity Page

1. Show Chart 4.

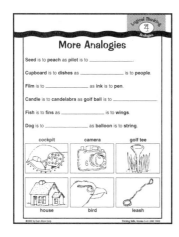

2. Have students name the relationship between each complete pair of words. Then have them choose a pictured object at the bottom of the page that completes the second pair of words in the same way.

3. Distribute the activity page, *Writing Analogies,* found on page 41.

4. Read with the class the information about using colons (or dots) to take the place of words in analogies.

5. Ask several students to rewrite the analogies on the chart using colons to replace the words *is to* and *as.*

6. Have students complete the activity page.

Extending the Skill

Have students rewrite the analogies on the chart using the first pair of words and supplying a new pair of words for the second half. For example:

fish : fins :: human : legs

Click and drag words to complete the analogies correctly.

More Analogies

Seed is to peach as pilot is to _____.

Cupboard is to dishes as _____ is to people.

Film is to _____ as ink is to pen.

Candle is to candelabra as golf ball is to _____.

Fish is to fins as _____ is to wings.

Dog is to _____ as balloon is to string.

cockpit

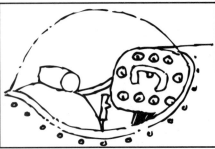

camera

golf tee

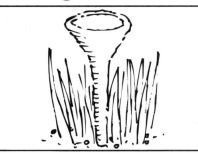

house

bird

leash

Name _____

Writing Analogies

Dots are used to take the place of the connecting words in an analogy. Two dots are often written in place of the words *is to*. Four dots mean *as*.

For example:

Poster is to wall as stamp is to envelope.

Can be written:

poster : wall : : stamp : envelope

Rewrite the first three examples with dots in place of the words.

1. **Page** is to **book** as **bone** is to **body**.

_____

2. **Dime** is to **money** as **German** is to **language**.

_____

3. **Blood** is to **vein** as **water** is to **aqueduct**.

_____

Write two analogies using dots in place of the words. You may invent your own or use your favorite ones from the analogy picture chart.

1. _____

2. _____

©2002 by Evan-Moor Corp.   Thinking Skills, Grades 5–6 • EMC 5303

Dark, Cold Night/Bright, Hot Day

Introducing the Skill

1. Show one dilapidated, used black crayon and one pristine, unused white crayon.

2. Ask students to explain the relationship between the two crayons.

   long/short new/old white/black fresh/spoiled

3. Guide students to the generalization that the two are **opposites**. Each pair of words describing their relationship is an example of opposites.

Using the Chart and Activity Page

1. Show Chart 5.

2. Distribute the activity page, *Opposite Is a Relationship,* found on page 44. Students will use the activity page to record their responses to the chart.

3. Have students list all the opposites generated by studying the pictures on the chart.

4. Explain that being opposite is a relationship. Ask students to use the pairs of opposites they made to create analogies. For example:

   fluffy : sleek :: sleeping : awake

5. Hopefully, someone will articulate the fact that it doesn't matter which opposite pairs are used in the analogy because the relationship of all the word pairs is the same.

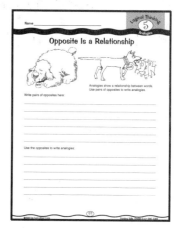

Extending the Skill

1. Divide your students into four teams.

2. Each team writes the name of an object in the classroom.

3. The names are passed on to the next team. The second team adds a word that has a relationship to the first. *(For example, if the first word is "paper," the second team might write "notebook.")*

4. The word pair is passed on. The third team writes the next part of the analogy. *(paper : notebook :: book)*

5. The fourth team adds the final word to complete the analogy. *(paper : notebook :: book : bookcase)*

6. Read and discuss the analogies at the end of the session.

CD Tips

Click in the text box and keyboard opposite pairs.

42

Dark, Cold Night
Bright, Hot Day

Think of all the ways that these two dogs represent opposites.

Opposite Is a Relationship

Analogies show a relationship between words. Use pairs of opposites to write analogies.

Write pairs of opposites here:

_____

_____

_____

_____

_____

_____

Use the opposites to write analogies:

_____

_____

_____

_____

_____

_____

_____

Thinking Skills, Grades 5–6 • EMC 5303

At the Zoo

Introducing the Skill

1. If your students have not had experience using a matrix to solve a logic problem, draw one on the chalkboard or project it from the CD or overhead projector.

2. Explain how the rows and columns are labeled.

	1	2	3	4
Lions				
Monkeys				
Zebras				
Giraffes				

Each row is labeled for one of the animals in the zoo. Each column represents the order in which the animals were visited.

3. Point out that the matrix is used to record information found in the clues and ultimately to answer the initial question.

*An **X** in a box means that choice could not be correct. There can only be one correct box in each row and in each column. Correct choices are marked with a **yes**.*

Using the Chart and Activity Page

1. Show Chart 6.

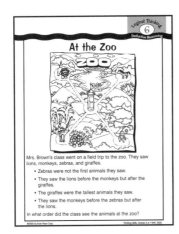

2. Work together to fill in the matrix and logically determine the order in which the animals were visited.

Read the clue: *Zebras were not the first animal they saw.*

Record the information: *Put an **X** in zebra box 1.*

Read the clue: *They saw the lions before the monkeys, but after the giraffes.*

Record the information: *The lions can't be first or last. Put an **X** in lion boxes 1 and 4. The monkeys can't be first. Put an **X** in monkey box 1. This leaves only one box open for first—the giraffe. Put **yes** in giraffe box 1 and **X** the rest of the boxes in the giraffe row.*

Read the clue: *The giraffes were the tallest animal.*

Record the information: This clue doesn't give any information that helps to answer the question.

Read the clue: *They saw the monkeys before the zebras but after the lions.*

Record the information: *The monkeys can't be last. Put an **X** in monkey box 4. This leaves only one box—zebras. Put **yes** in zebra box 4 and an **X** in all other boxes in that row. So the lions and monkeys are 2nd and 3rd. Since the monkeys are after the lions, put **yes** in lion box 2 and **yes** in monkey box 3.*

3. Students complete the activity page, *New Clothes*, found on page 47.

4. Help them set up a properly labeled matrix before beginning.

Click and drag the *X* and *yes* into the correct boxes to complete the matrix.

Thinking Skills, Grades 5–6 • EMC 5303

At the Zoo

Mrs. Brown's class went on a field trip to the zoo. They saw lions, monkeys, zebras, and giraffes.

- Zebras were not the first animals they saw.

- They saw the lions before the monkeys but after the giraffes.

- The giraffes were the tallest animals they saw.

- They saw the monkeys before the zebras but after the lions.

In what order did the class see the animals at the zoo?

Name _____

New Clothes

Mrs. Hubbard has just come back from a shopping trip for her four children. She bought each child the outfit they had asked for. But when Mother Hubbard emptied her shopping bag, she couldn't remember who got what outfit.

Here are the facts that she knows:

1. The four children that requested clothing are Terry, Sean, Bobbie, and Sammy.

2. Mrs. Hubbard bought a blue short-sleeved shirt and blue shorts; a pair of jeans and a plaid jacket; a long red dress; black tennis shoes and white socks.

3. Sammy wants to borrow the jacket tomorrow.

4. Sean hates anything in red.

5. Terry lost his only jacket at summer camp last week.

6. Bobbie never wears jeans.

7. Bobbie and Sammy share a closet.

8. Sammy and Sean have both just bought new tennis shoes and socks.

9. Bobbie already has a red dress.

10. Sean and Terry can wear each other's clothes.

Use a matrix and the data above to help Mrs. Hubbard give each child the outfit that he or she requested. When you have completed the matrix, write the name of each child beside the description of the clothing they should receive. Circle the number of any fact that is unnecessary to solve the problem.

- blue shirt and blue shorts   _____

- jeans and a plaid jacket   _____

- long red dress   _____

- black tennis shoes and white socks _____

Thinking Skills, Grades 5–6 • EMC 5303

The Bus Riders

Introducing the Skill

It is important to learn to organize information when trying to solve logic problems. Information can be recorded on a matrix as in Chart 6 or a diagram that allows thinkers to visualize the relationships between the clues that are given. As with any logic puzzle, it is important to read through all the clues before trying to solve the puzzle.

Using the Chart and Activity Page

1. Show Chart 7.

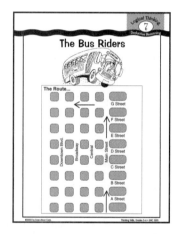

2. Distribute the activity page, *The Bus Riders,* found on page 50. This page gives the puzzle clues and a place to track the information given in the clues.

3. Guide the class through the clues. Write names of riders in the boxes at each stop if they got off at that stop, or put an *X* in the box to show that no one got off.

Here is the logical thinking used to solve the puzzle:

- None of the 10 students got off the bus at B & Main or at C & Main (clue 2), and all had left the bus before it reached G & Downtown Boulevard (clue 9). Put an *X* in the box by each of these stops.

- The first student to get off rode for three blocks (clue 2). Javiar was the first off the bus, and none of the others got off at this stop or the next stop (clue 3). Write *Javiar* in the box at D & Main and put an *X* in the box at E & Main.

- Carlos got off three blocks before Emil (clue 6), so Carlos must have gotten off at F & Main, and Emil at G & Broadway. Emil got off one stop after Alicia, so Alicia must have gotten off at G & Central. Write their names in the appropriate boxes.

- Maria got off the bus before Sam (clue 5). She didn't get off at G & Main, and Sam didn't get off at G & Broadway (clue 8), so Maria can only have left the bus at F & Main. Write her name in that box.

- There are five students left. To satisfy clue 1, twice as many students got off at G & Central as at G & Main. Putting clue 4 and clue 7 together, we know that Liz and Edward got off before Muhammad and Darice. Write *Liz and Edward* in the box at G & Main, and *Muhammad and Darice* in the box at G & Central.

- There are still not twice as many names in the box at G & Central. Sam is not yet placed. Write *Sam* in the box at G & Central to make four students at that stop, twice the number as at G & Main.

Drag the numbers by the students' names to the correct bus stops to show where they exited the bus.

(48)

The Bus Riders

The Route...

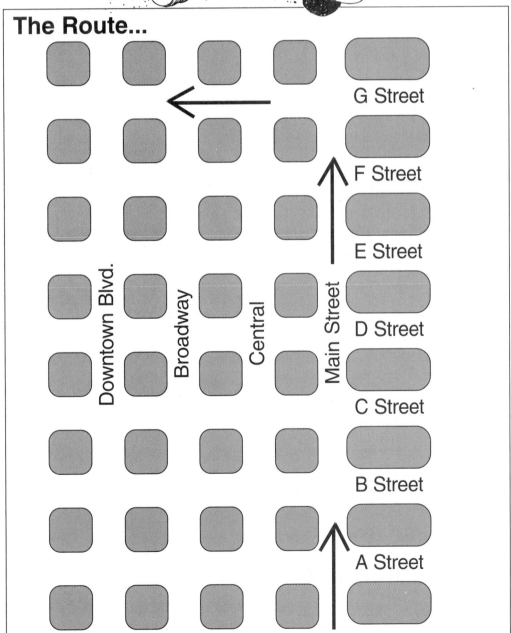

G Street

F Street

E Street

D Street

C Street

B Street

A Street

Downtown Blvd.

Broadway

Central

Main Street

The Bus Riders

After school, 10 students boarded Bus 141 at the corner of A Street & Main. The bus, which stops at every corner, proceeds up Main Street, first passing B Street, then C Street, and so on, turning left on G Street. The bus passes Central, Broadway, and Downtown Boulevard on its route.

Study the clues and then indicate where each of the 10 students got off the bus.

Clues:

1. Twice as many students got off the bus at G Street & Central than got off at G Street & Main.

2. The first student to get off rode for three blocks.

3. Javiar got off first. None of the others got off at his stop or at the next stop.

4. Liz and Edward got off at the same stop; Muhammad and Darice got off at the same stop.

5. Sam was still on the bus after Maria got off.

6. Carlos got off the bus three blocks before Emil. Emil got off one stop after Alicia.

7. Muhammad's stop was after Liz's stop.

8. Maria didn't get off the bus at G Street & Main. Sam didn't get off at G Street & Broadway.

9. All 10 students left the bus before it reached G Street & Downtown Boulevard.

The Students:

Javiar	Sam	Liz	Maria	Darice
Edward	Carlos	Muhammad	Emil	Alicia

The Stops:

A St. & Main		F St & Main.	
B St. & Main		G St. & Main	
C St. & Main		G St. & Central	
D St. & Main		G St. & Broadway	
E St. & Main		G St. & Downtown Blvd.	

Thinking Skills, Grades 5–6 • EMC 5303

State Trees

Introducing the Skill

Solving logic puzzles or answering questions using deductive reasoning doesn't always involve a matrix. Use Chart 8 as an example of the importance of using visual clues from the picture and clues in the written information together to ascertain specific facts.

Using the Chart and Activity Page

1. Show Chart 8.

2. As a class, read all of the clues.

3. Decide together which two clues contain information that can be recorded immediately.

    The Douglas fir is the first tree on the left. Label A—Douglas fir

    The redwood tree is only next to the live oak. Label G—redwood

    Label F—live oak

4. Go back and reread the other clues. Label the remaining trees.

5. Distribute the student activity page, *State Tree Matrix,* on page 53.

6. Remind students to place an *X* on the grid when they find that a tree cannot be the symbol of one of the states. They should write the word *yes* when a tree and state match is found.

Click in the label boxes to keyboard the tree names.

Thinking Skills, Grades 5–6 • EMC 5303

State Trees

A   B   C   D   E   F   G

Seven state trees grow in the forest pictured on the chart. Follow the clues and identify the trees.

- The one-leaf piñon tree is next to the American elm and the red maple.

- The Sabal palmetto is between the red maple and the live oak.

- The Douglas fir is the first tree on the left.

- The redwood tree is only next to the live oak.

Name _____

State Tree Matrix

In our country, each state has chosen a special tree. Use the clues and the matrix to match the following states and their trees.

- Rhode Island's tree is two words. The first letter of the first word for the state and the tree are the same.

- California's tree is named for the color of its trunk.

- The American elm is not the state tree of Florida, Nevada, or Georgia.

- Oregon's tree is a popular Christmas tree that begins with a person's name.

- The name of South Carolina's tree begins with the same letter as the state.

- The one-leaf piñon tree represents a state that borders California.

	redwood	one-leaf piñon	American elm	live oak	Douglas fir	Sabal palmetto	red maple
Oregon							
Massachusetts, Nebraska, & North Dakota							
Rhode Island							
California							
Florida & South Carolina							
Nevada							
Georgia							

Thinking Skills, Grades 5–6 • EMC 5303

Syllogisms

Introducing the Skill

1. Write the word *syllogism* on the chalkboard and define it for the class:

   A syllogism is a form of reasoning that consists of two statements that are assumed to be true and a conclusion based on those statements. Sometimes the conclusion is valid or true; sometimes it is not.

   > *All people have the ability to think.*

   > *All children are people.*

   > *Therefore, all children have the ability to think.*

2. Explain that the famous Greek philosopher, Aristotle, developed syllogisms. Syllogisms follow strict rules or guidelines.

   - A syllogisms has three main words or ideas. Each statement in the syllogism uses two of the three words. Each set of the two words can be used only once. For example, the three main words in the syllogism below are *rattlesnakes, reptiles,* and *biting creatures.*

     > *All rattlesnakes are reptiles.*

     > *Some rattlesnakes are biting creatures.*

     > *Therefore, some reptiles are biting creatures.*

   - If qualifying words, such as *all, everyone, none, few, some, often,* and *many* are used in the first two sections, the correct matching word must be used in the conclusion. Share the following example of an invalid syllogism caused by qualifying words that do not match.

     > *Some students in the school have a cold.*

     > *Cold germs spread quickly in schools and offices.*

     > *Therefore, all students in class will get a cold.*

   What makes this syllogism invalid? *(The word **all** in the third statement implies that everyone will get a cold. Just because cold germs spread quickly, not all people who are exposed to cold germs get a cold.)*

   How could the third sentence be changed to make a valid conclusion? *(The qualifying words in the first and third sentences should match. If **some** is used in the first sentence, it must be used in the conclusion—Therefore, **some** students in class will get a cold.)*

Using the Chart and Activity Page

1. Show Chart 9.

2. As a class, read the syllogisms and supply valid conclusions.

3. Distribute the activity page, *Syllogisms,* found on page 56.

4. Students choose the better conclusion for each syllogism.

Extending the Skill

Challenge students to write their own syllogisms.

Click on the line to keyboard the conclusion for each syllogism.

Thinking Skills, Grades 5–6 • EMC 5303

Syllogisms

The last line for each syllogism is missing.

What should the last line be?

1. All children like ice cream.

   All girls are children.

   Therefore, _____.

2. All cats are purring animals.

   All feline Persians are cats.

   Therefore, _____.

3. All birds have feathers.

   All chickens are birds.

   Therefore, _____.

4. All stars are in the sky.

   The sun is a star.

   Therefore, _____.

5. All apples are fruit.

   No insects are fruit.

   Therefore, _____.

Syllogisms

Long ago in Greece, great importance was placed on ideas and how people thought. Aristotle, a famous thinker, invented syllogisms (sil-uh-jiz´-ums).

A syllogism has three sections. Facts are given in the first two parts. The third part is a new idea taken from the facts in the first two sections.

Example: All people have two eyes.

All children are people.

Therefore, all children have two eyes.

Read the following syllogisms and place an **X** in front of the better conclusion for each one.

All roses have thorns.

Some flowers are roses.

_____ Therefore, some flowers have thorns.

_____ Therefore, be careful when you pick roses.

All chairs are furniture.

Some chairs are made from wood.

_____ Therefore, chairs are furniture.

_____ Therefore, some furniture is made from wood.

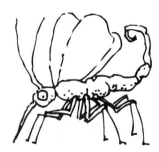

All mosquitoes are insects.

Some mosquitoes are biting creatures.

_____ Therefore, stay away from mosquitoes.

_____ Therefore, some insects are biting creatures.

Thinking Skills, Grades 5–6 • EMC 5303

Silly Syllogisms

Introducing the Skill

Explain to students that the two premises or statements in a syllogism do not have to be true, but they must logically support the conclusion.

All fifth-graders love turnips.

Turnips are root vegetables.

Therefore, all fifth-graders love root vegetables.

Even though this syllogism is valid—the two premises or statements logically support the conclusion—it is not true. (All fifth-graders do not necessarily love turnips.)

Using the Chart and Activity Page

1. Show Chart 10.

2. As a class, evaluate the syllogisms to determine if they are valid.

3. Distribute the activity page, *Is It Valid?*, found on page 59.

4. Students practice identifying valid and invalid syllogisms.

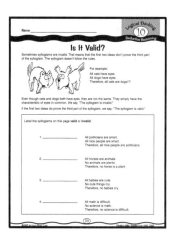

Extending the Skill

1. Students choose a product.

2. They write a syllogism about the product.

All athletes need Go-Power.

Some fifth-graders are athletes.

Therefore, some fifth-graders need Go-Power.

Click on the picture beside each syllogism to see if it is valid or invalid.

Thinking Skills, Grades 5–6 • EMC 5303

Silly Syllogisms

Syllogisms don't have to be true. They can be very silly as long as the syllogism rules are followed.

Check to see if these silly syllogisms are valid.

All frogs are green.
All green things are ugly.
Therefore, all frogs are ugly.

All movies are exciting.
Some scary things are movies.
Therefore, some exciting things are scary.

All baby pigs are squealing animals.
All baby pigs are cute.
Therefore, all squealing animals are cute.

All giraffes have spots.
No giraffes are camels.
Therefore, no camels have spots.

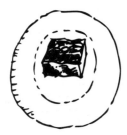

All fudge is sticky.
Some sticky things are yucky.
Therefore, some fudge is yucky.

Is It Valid?

Sometimes syllogisms are invalid. That means that the first two ideas don't prove the third part of the syllogism. The syllogism doesn't follow the rules.

For example:

All cats have eyes.
All dogs have eyes.
Therefore, all cats are dogs!?!

Even though cats and dogs both have eyes, they are not the same. They simply have the characteristic of eyes in common. We say, "The syllogism is invalid."

If the first two ideas do prove the third part of the syllogism, we say, "The syllogism is valid."

Label the syllogisms on this page **valid** or **invalid**.

1. _____   All politicians are smart.
                          All nice people are smart.
                          Therefore, all nice people are politicians.

2. _____   All horses are animals.
                          No animals are plants.
                          Therefore, no horse is a plant.

3. _____   All babies are cute.
                          No cute things cry.
                          Therefore, no babies cry.

4. _____   All math is difficult.
                          No science is math.
                          Therefore, no science is difficult.

Thinking Skills, Grades 5–6 • EMC 5303

Introducing the Skill

This chart requires that students apply deductive reasoning to factual information. Remind students to read through the entire list of facts on the activity page before marking any spaces on the grid.

Using the Chart and Activity Page

1. Show Chart 11.

2. Distribute the activity page, *Famous Mountains Blow Their Tops,* found on page 62.

3. Students read the facts on the activity page, use geography they know or look up, and mark the grid to locate each of the volcanoes.

Extending the Skill

Students research these interesting volcanoes. Other volcanoes may be added to Professor Fog's chart as students do more research.

Drag *X* or *yes* into each of the boxes to complete the matrix.

Thinking Skills, Grades 5–6 • EMC 5303

Famous Mountains Blow Their Tops

Where are Krakatau, Mount Pelee, Mount Vesuvius, Mount Pinatubo, and Mount St. Helens?

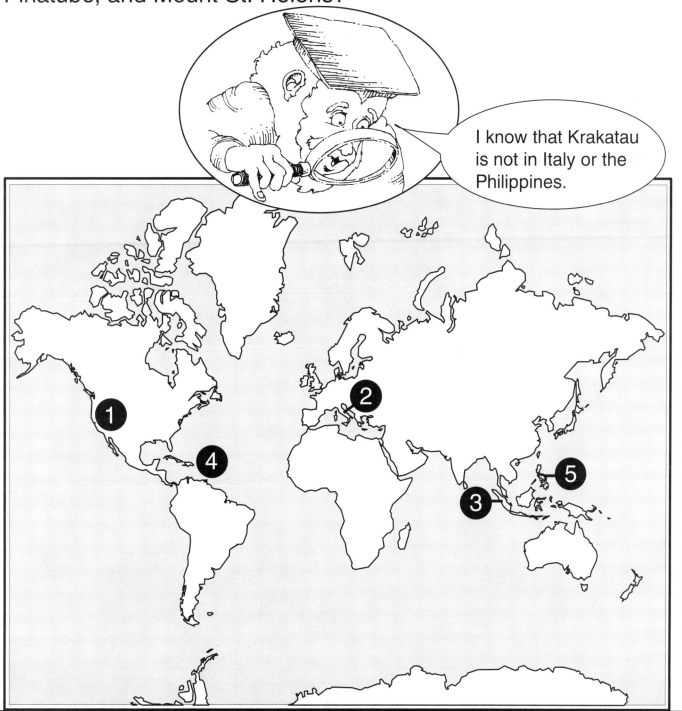

I know that Krakatau is not in Italy or the Philippines.

Famous Mountains Blow Their Tops

It's not easy to lose a volcano, but Professor Fog is having trouble identifying the volcanoes marked on his map. He remembers only one fact for sure, but he has made a series of notes about all the volcanoes. Some of the notes were made before he completed his research, so in each pair of statements, only one is true. Choose either **A** or **B** for each number. Help Professor Fog find the true statements and prepare for his worldwide volcano tour. Mark the information from each correct statement on the grid, and then locate the volcanoes on the map.

1. **A.** Mt. Vesuvius is in Italy, and Mt. Pelee is in Martinique.
   B. Mt. Vesuvius is in Indonesia, and Mt. Pelee is in Italy.
   (Read on. There isn't enough information here.)

2. **A.** Krakatau is in Indonesia, and Mt. St. Helens is in the United States of America.
   B. Krakatau is in Italy, and Mt. St. Helens is in Martinique.
   Hint: Krakatau is not in Italy or the Philippines, so mark an **X** for Krakatau on the grid below Italy and the Philippines. Now go back to 2. Which statement is correct? Write on the chart where it belongs. Now you are on your way and on your own.

3. **A.** Mt. Pinatubo is in the Philippines, and Mt. St. Helens is in the United States of America.
   B. Mt. Pelee is in Italy, and Krakatau is in the United States of America.

	Italy	Indonesia	USA	Martinique	Philippines
Krakatau					
Mt. Vesuvius					
Mt. St. Helens					
Mt. Pelee					
Mt. Pinatubo					

Thinking Skills, Grades 5–6 • EMC 5303

Introducing the Skill

1. Tell students that the United States of America does not mine more zinc than Canada.

2. Using that one fact, students will eliminate incorrect statements and locate deposits of six important minerals.

Using the Chart and Activity Page

1. Show Chart 12.

2. Distribute the activity page, *Join the Pick and Shovel Club,* found on page 65.

3. Students read each statement carefully and eliminate one statement in each pair.

4. Then have students record the information from each correct statement on the grid.

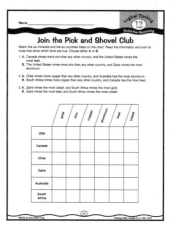

Extending the Skill

Have students find out the different uses of each of the minerals on the chart.

Click on the pick and shovel icon to see the beginning fact. (The United States of America does not mine more zinc than Canada.) Drag the number for the country to the correct mineral.

Thinking Skills, Grades 5–6 • EMC 5303

Join the Pick and Shovel Club

Get Ready, Get Set, Dig!
Which country mines the most?

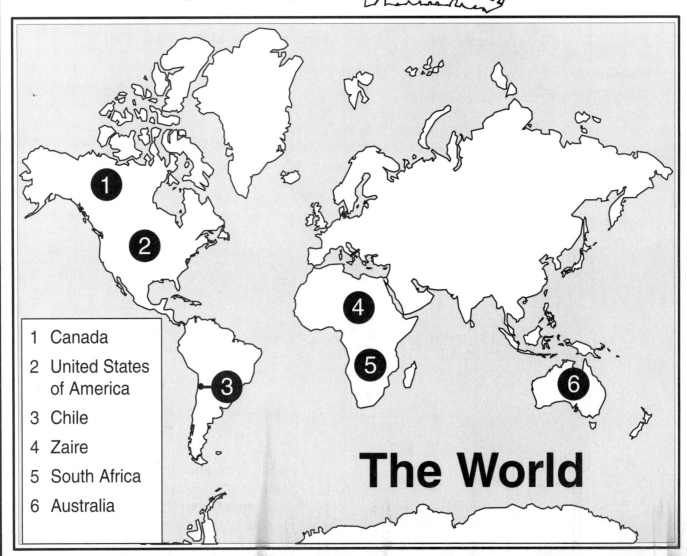

1 Canada
2 United States of America
3 Chile
4 Zaire
5 South Africa
6 Australia

The World

Join the Pick and Shovel Club

Match the six minerals and the six countries listed on the chart. Read the information and look for clues that show which facts are true. Choose either **A** or **B**.

1. **A.** Canada mines more zinc than any other country, and the United States mines the most lead.
   B. The United States mines more zinc than any other country, and Zaire mines the most aluminum.

2. **A.** Chile mines more copper than any other country, and Australia has the most aluminum.
   B. South Africa mines more copper than any other country, and Canada has the most lead.

3. **A.** Zaire mines the most cobalt, and South Africa mines the most gold.
   B. Zaire mines the most lead, and South Africa mines the most cobalt.

	gold	zinc	copper	aluminum	lead	cobalt
USA						
Canada						
Chile						
Zaire						
Australia						
South Africa						

Thinking Skills, Grades 5–6 • EMC 5303

Speedy Delivery

Introducing the Skill

1. Review with students strategies they have developed to solve matrix logic puzzles.

2. Explain that students begin with a labeled matrix. In this activity, they will label the matrix before filling it out.

Using the Chart and Activity Page

1. Show Chart 13.

2. Distribute the activity page, *Speedy Delivery,* on page 68.

3. Have students read the clues on the chart carefully and then label the matrix.

4. Discuss the labels and make sure that students' matrixes are labeled correctly.

5. Have students complete the grid.

Extending the Skill

Have students name a new delivery person. Expect them to follow the pattern of the other delivery people—*synonym for fast or quick + name beginning with the same initial consonant.*

After students have completed their matrixes, click on delivery people's names to confirm the correct answers.

Thinking Skills, Grades 5–6 • EMC 5303

Speedy Delivery

The Speedy Express Bicycle Delivery Service is known for its quick and reliable service. Meet its seven fantastic delivery people.

Read the clues below to find the number of deliveries that each delivery person made last Friday.

Clues:

1. The fewest deliveries that anyone made is 32.

2. Three delivery persons made deliveries in the 30s, two in the 40s, one in the 50s, and one in the 60s.

3. One of the women made 38 deliveries.

4. Swift Suzie made the most deliveries—20 more than Quick Quincy.

5. The number of deliveries for the ready, nimble, and agile delivery persons are in the 30s.

6. Fleet Florence made one more delivery than Nimble Ned, who made 39 deliveries.

7. Quick Quincy made 10 more deliveries than Agile Avery.

8. Prompt Peter made 11 more deliveries than Fleet Florence.

Speedy Delivery

Label this matrix with information from the chart. Begin by listing the names of the delivery persons down the left side. As you read the clues, fill in the labels across the top. Each label will be a number of deliveries. Then reread the clues and fill in the grid.

 Thinking Skills, Grades 5–6 • EMC 5303

Holiday Shopping

Introducing the Skill

In this matrix puzzle, students will work with three variables. Explain that the heavy black line down the center of the grid divides the money variable from the store variable. Each member of the Sutter family will have a *yes* in both the money and the store sections.

Using the Chart and Activity Page

1. Show Chart 14.

2. Distribute the activity page, *Holiday Shopping,* on page 71.

3. Depending on the level of your students, work together or independently to solve the problem.

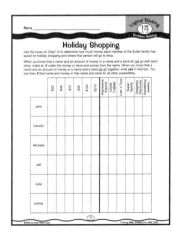

Extending the Skill

Each member of the Sutter family must buy a gift for each of the other family members. Have students choose one member of the family and, using the amount of money saved and the store where shopping was done, tell what gifts that person bought and how much each gift cost.

After students have completed their matrixes, drag store names under each person's coin purse, and keyboard the amount saved in the appropriate coin purse.

Thinking Skills, Grades 5–6 • EMC 5303

Holiday Shopping

The members of the Sutter family have saved all year for their annual holiday shopping spree. Each family member will go to a different store. Use the clues below to find out how much money each person has saved and in which store each person will shop.

John   Carolyn   Michelle   Emma   Julie   Jeff

Clues:

1. If you add the money that John and Carolyn have saved together, you get $120.

2. If you add the money that Michelle and Emma have saved together, you get $120.

3. Julie has saved more money than Jeff.

4. The person who saved $120 is going to Impressive Imports.

5. Michelle is going to a store whose name begins with the letter **L**.

6. Julie is going to a store that specializes in gold bracelets and diamond cuff links.

7. Neither Carolyn nor Emma is going to Larry's Luggage.

8. The person going to Lots 'o Toys has more money than the person going to Delightful Discounts or Larry's Luggage, but less money than the person going to Super Sports.

9. Emma has saved $48.

10. Carolyn is going to Super Sports to do her shopping.

Holiday Shopping

Use the clues on Chart 14 to determine how much money each member of the Sutter family has saved for holiday shopping and where that person will go to shop.

When you know that a name and an amount of money or a name and a store do <u>not</u> go with each other, make an **X** under the money or store and across from the name. When you know that a name and an amount of money or a name and a store <u>do</u> go together, write **yes** in that box. You can then **X** that name and money or that name and store for all other possibilities.

	$25	$48	$72	$95	$120	$210	Impressive Imports	Larry's Luggage	Lots 'o Toys	Super Sports	Delightful Discounts	Something Jewelry
John												
Carolyn												
Michelle												
Jeff												
Julie												
Emma												

Thinking Skills, Grades 5–6 • EMC 5303

The Candy Store

Introducing the Skill

1. This is a difficult problem. You may want to read each of the clues as a class and ask students to suggest strategies they might use to solve the problem, before actually beginning to solve the problem. You could offer this suggestion:

   It helps to think about relationships between the candies. Equations are a way to express relationships. For example, after reading Clue 1, I know:

   giant gumdrop = peanut butter cup – 2¢
   giant gumdrop = licorice – 7¢

2. Divide the class into small groups.

Using the Chart and Activity Page

1. Show Chart 15.

2. Give each group two copies of the activity page on page 74, small pieces of paper on which to write + and – signs, and coins.

3. Have groups explain their problem-solving strategies and solutions to the class.

Here's one way the reasoning might proceed:

Step 1: Begin by figuring out how many different prices there will be. Nine different kinds of candy were mentioned. Since three of the candies cost 15¢ (Clue 5) and there are two candies at each of the other prices, the other six must have three different prices. So there are four different prices for the candies.

Step 2: Compare the prices of the candies with equations.
1. *giant gumdrop = peanut butter cup – 2¢*
2. *giant gumdrop = licorice rope – 7¢*
3. *caramel = taffy + 2¢*
4. *caramel = gummy frog – 7¢*
5. *chocolate bar = fruit roll + 2¢*
6. *chocolate bar = peanut butter cup + 7¢*
7. *lollipop = caramel + 7¢*

Step 3: Solve the equations you can. Using Clue 6 (taffy costs 6¢), you can solve equations 3, 4, and 7 and find the price for these candies:

taffy = 6¢	gummy frog = 15¢
caramel = 8¢	lollipop = 15¢

Step 4: Look at the remaining equations. Compare the two different equations for the giant gumdrop with the two equations for the chocolate bar, and you find the following equalities:

   peanut butter cup – 2¢ = licorice rope – 7¢
   fruit roll + 2¢ = peanut butter cup + 7¢
   So: peanut butter cup = licorice rope – 5¢

Put these equalities together and you have: fruit roll = (licorice rope – 5¢) + 5¢ **or** the peanut butter cup = fruit roll. Since the licorice rope and the fruit roll have the same price, they must both be the fourth price, whatever it is. Only one more candy is needed for 15¢, 8¢, and 6¢.

Step 5: The clues say that the chocolate bar = fruit roll + 2¢. The chocolate bar must have a price of 15¢ because: If it were 6¢, the fruit roll and the licorice rope would both be 4¢. Since the gumdrop = the licorice rope – 7¢, that isn't possible. If the chocolate bar were 8¢, the fruit roll and the licorice rope would cost 6¢. Taffy already costs 6¢, and only two candies can cost 6¢, so that isn't possible.

Step 6: The fruit roll and the licorice rope must cost 13¢. Finally, the peanut butter cup = 8¢, and the giant gumdrop = 6¢.

After students have completed their activity pages, click on each candy to show the correct answers.

Thinking Skills, Grades 5–6 • EMC 5303

The Candy Store

The candy store has lots of
different treats, but Emil can't
find the signs that tell how
much each one costs. Can you
use these clues to help him?

1 Giant gumdrops cost 2¢ less than peanut butter cups
and 7¢ less than licorice ropes.

2 Caramels cost 2¢ more than taffy and 7¢ less than
gummy frogs.

3 A chocolate bar costs 2¢ more than a fruit roll and
7¢ more than a peanut butter cup.

4 A lollipop costs 7¢ more than a caramel.

5 Three of the candies cost 15¢ each. There are two
candies at each other price.

6 A piece of taffy costs only 6¢.

Name _____

The Candy Store

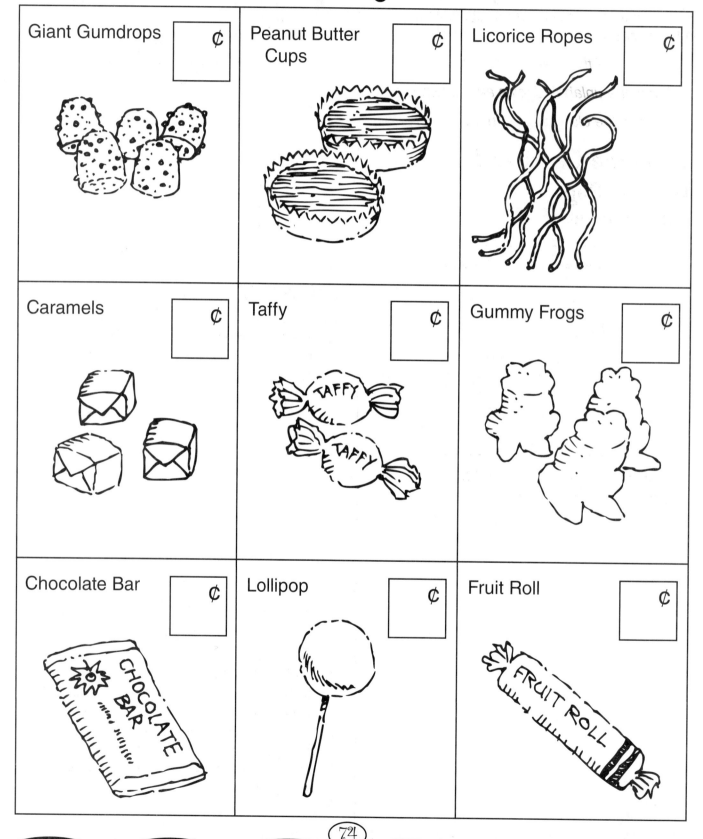

| Giant Gumdrops | ☐ ¢ | Peanut Butter Cups | ☐ ¢ | Licorice Ropes | ☐ ¢ |

| Caramels | ☐ ¢ | Taffy | ☐ ¢ | Gummy Frogs | ☐ ¢ |

| Chocolate Bar | ☐ ¢ | Lollipop | ☐ ¢ | Fruit Roll | ☐ ¢ |

74

The Collectors' Club

Introducing the Skill

Review the steps students should follow to solve a matrix puzzle.

Read all of the clues.

Label the unlabeled rows and columns.

Reread the clues and fill in the information.

Using the Chart and Activity Page

1. Show Chart 16.

2. Distribute the activity page, *The Collectors' Club,* on page 77.

3. Students read the information on the chart and use it to complete the matrix on the activity page.

Extending the Skill

Have students find out more about Lou Gehrig, Babe Ruth, Honus Wagner, and Ty Cobb. Add to this list of old-time baseball heroes.

Click on the name above each notebook to learn more about the famous baseball players. After students have completed their matrixes, click on each notebook to change it to the appropriate color and check the number of cards each boy collected.

Thinking Skills, Grades 5–6 • EMC 5303

The Collectors' Club

Four sixth-grade boys formed the Baseball Card Collectors' Club. They nicknamed themselves after famous old-time baseball players. They store their baseball cards in different-colored notebooks. Can you use the clues to determine the color of each boy's book and the number of cards that each book contains?

Clues:

1. Honus has 1,205 baseball cards.

2. Ty has a black notebook.

3. Neither Lou nor Babe has the green book.

4. Lou has the red book.

5. The blue book contains the most cards.

6. One of the boys with a Yankee player nickname has the fewest number of cards, and the other has the largest number of cards.

As a New York Yankee, Babe Ruth twice hit three home runs in a World Series game.

Ty Cobb played in Detroit and Philadelphia. He was one of the first five players selected to the Baseball Hall of Fame in 1936.

Lou Gehrig, nicknamed the Iron Horse, signed a contract to play with the Yankees when he was attending Columbia University.

Honus Wagner earned his nickname "The Flying Dutchman" when he played for Pittsburg. He was the league leader in stolen bases five times.

Name _____

The Collectors' Club Clues

Read the clues on the chart. Label the unlabeled rows and columns on the matrix. When you know that a boy and a color or a boy and a number of cards do <u>not</u> go with each other, make an **X** under the color or number of cards and across from the boy. When you know that a boy and a color or a boy and a number of cards <u>do</u> go together, write **yes** in that box.

				315	720	1205	2403

Thinking Skills, Grades 5–6 • EMC 5303

The Cake Walk

Introducing the Skill

Complete several matrix problems in which the grids are labeled before asking students to label a blank matrix like the one in this lesson.

Using the Chart and Activity Page

1. Show Chart 17.

2. Distribute the activity page, *Who Baked It?*, found on page 80.

3. Students read the information on the chart and label the matrix.

4. Then the students fill in the matrix to solve the puzzle.

Extending the Skill

If your students have never experienced a cake walk, stage one in your classroom. Classroom coupons such as "10 Minutes Free Reading Time" could be substituted for cakes.

After students have completed their matrixes, drag each cake into the appropriate box. Keyboard the student bakers' names in the appropriate box.

Thinking Skills, Grades 5–6 • EMC 5303

The Cake Walk

Lindy, Sam, Peter, and Penny each plan to make a cake for the cake walk at the school carnival. Each student has been selected to represent their class—Mr. Call's class, Mrs. Ryan's class, Mrs. Kehl's class, and Mrs. Smith's class. Use the clues to determine what kind of cake each student will make and which class they represent.

Angelic Angel   Granny's Apple   Precious Pound   Chocolate Madness

Who Baked It?

Read the clues below. Label the rows and the columns on the matrix. When you know that a student and a cake or a student and a class do <u>not</u> go with each other, make an **X** under the cake or the class across from the person. When you know that a student and a cake or a student and a class <u>do</u> go together, write **yes** in that box.

Clues:

1. Sam is not making a chocolate or a pound cake.

2. Lindy represents Mrs. Kehl's class.

3. One of the girls is going to make her grandmother's apple cake recipe.

4. The student making the Precious Pound cake represents Mrs. Kehl's class.

5. Sam is making an angel food cake and represents the class listed immediately after Penny's class.

(80)

Bug Trivia

Introducing the Skill

Explain to students that the information they have may not directly answer the questions they are asked. They will need to interpret the information they have and then choose a reasonable answer.

Using the Chart and Activity Page

1. Show Chart 18.

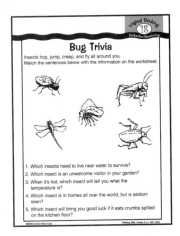

2. Distribute the activity page, *Bug Trivia*, found on page 83.

3. Students read the information on the activity page and then tell which statements on the chart apply to each bug.

Extending the Skill

Make an insect encyclopedia. Each student chooses an insect and finds information about their buggy friend. The information is written below a drawing of the insect. The pages may be arranged alphabetically in a loose-leaf notebook. Other pages may be added during the year.

Drag the insect name to answer each question.

81

Bug Trivia

Insects hop, jump, creep, and fly all around you.
Match the questions below with the insect names and statements on the worksheet.

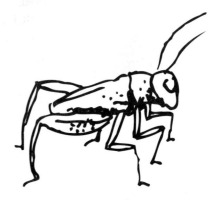

1. Which insects need to live near water to survive?

2. Which insect is an unwelcome visitor in your garden?

3. When it's hot, which insect will tell you what the temperature is?

4. Which insect is in homes all over the world, but is seldom seen?

5. Which insect will bring you good luck if it eats crumbs spilled on the kitchen floor?

Bug Trivia

Read about these interesting insects. On the lines by their names, write one or more of the sentence numbers from the chart.

The Black Fly _____
Black flies lay their eggs in streams and rivers. When they hatch, the wormlike larvae attach themselves to rocks in the water. They filter food from the water that flows by. Later, they form cocoons. When they become adults, they fly away in swarms, biting animals and people.

The Treehopper _____
This insect is hard to find because it looks like a thorn or part of the plant. After the eggs hatch, the nymphs suck out the plant juices.

The Dragonfly _____
These flying machines have long, slender wings. They hover over streams and ponds hunting for mosquito larvae. Dragonflies scoop up victims with their legs. With their hinged lower jaws, they can snap up tadpoles, small fish, and insects.

The Cricket _____
There are many kinds of crickets. Finding a cricket in your house is supposed to bring good luck. If you hear a snowy tree cricket when the weather is hot, add 40 to the number of times it chirps in 15 seconds. That will be the approximate Fahrenheit temperature.

The Cockroach _____
Cockroaches eat almost anything including paper, soap, and glue. They are night creatures that scurry out of sight when there is light, air currents, or sounds. They live in houses all over the world.

Thinking Skills, Grades 5–6 • EMC 5303

Decisions

Introducing the Skill

As students work with their problem-solving skills, it is valuable to have them consider real problems that affect them. This chart focuses on a problem that faces every individual in today's society.

Using the Chart and Activity Page

1. Show Chart 19.

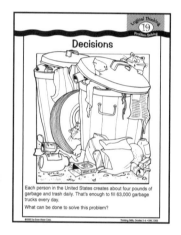

2. As a class, read and discuss the question on the chart. Record possible solutions on the chalkboard or a chart.

3. Using the activity page, *Totaling Up the Trash,* on page 86, do a survey to find out what trash is produced each day in your classroom.

4. Look at the board or chart showing your original suggested solutions. Ask students if, after doing the survey of their classroom trash, they would like to add to or revise their solutions.

Click in the text box to keyboard students' responses.

Extending the Skill

1. Students report the results of the classroom recycling campaign in an article for a local newspaper.

2. Students develop recycling recommendations for the school based on their experience in the classroom.

Some Important Facts

One half of the garbage that Americans throw out could be recycled. *Recycling* means reusing the waste instead of throwing it out. If we did recycle the half that we could, every day we would recycle enough garbage to fill a football stadium from top to bottom.

- Recycling a six-pack of aluminum cans can save enough energy to drive a car five miles.

- One recycled aluminum can saves enough electricity to operate a television for three hours.

- Making a tin can from recycled steel takes only ¼ of the energy needed to make the same can from new steel.

- Recycling one six-foot stack of newspapers saves the life of one 35-foot-tall tree.

84

Decisions

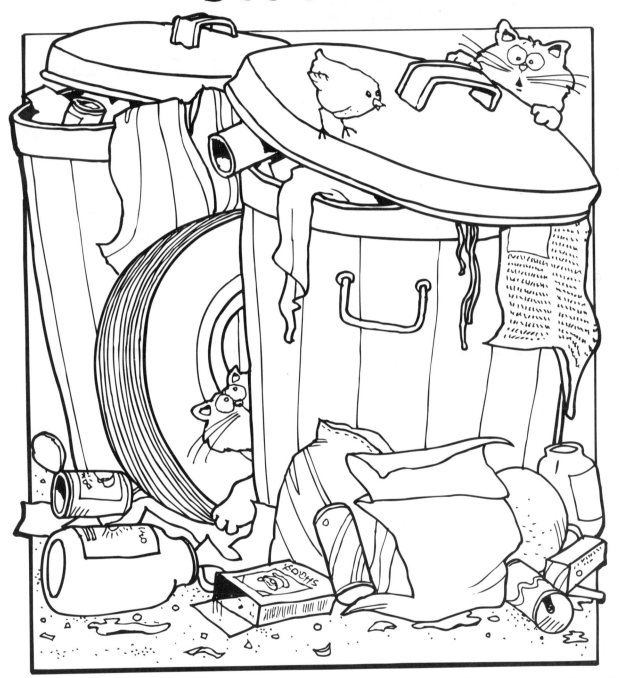

Each person in the United States creates about four pounds of garbage and trash daily. That's enough to fill 63,000 garbage trucks every day.

What can be done to solve this problem?

Name _____

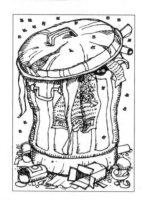

Totaling Up the Trash

Do a survey to find out what trash is produced each day in your classroom. For several days in a row, go to the trash cans around your room and get to know your trash. List each item and what the item is made of. Then indicate whether the item can be recycled. This will help you see what your class can do to reduce trash.

Item	What is it made of?	Can it be recycled?

Thinking Skills, Grades 5–6 • EMC 5303

Number Patterns

Introducing the Skill

1. Write this number pattern on the chalkboard.

   0   5   7   12   14   19

2. Ask students what number would come next. Help them to analyze the pattern. Ask questions like:

   What is the relationship of the first two numbers?

   What is the relationship of the next two?

   Are either of those relationships repeated?

3. Explain that +5, +2 is the rule for the pattern.

Using the Chart and Activity Page

1. Show Chart 20.

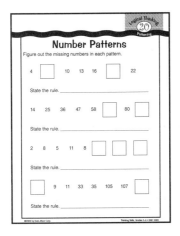

2. Give students a chance to solve each of the number patterns on the chart. If necessary, guide them to solutions with leading questions.

3. Have them state the rule for each pattern.

4. Distribute the activity page, *More Number Patterns,* found on page 89.

5. Students solve the number patterns, state the pattern rules, and create a number pattern of their own.

6. Share the strategies that students used to solve the problems.

Extending the Skill

Start each morning with a number pattern. Reinforce math skills as you help students sharpen their logical thinking.

Click on the blanks to keyboard answers. Then keyboard the rule under each pattern.

Thinking Skills, Grades 5–6 • EMC 5303

Number Patterns

Figure out the missing numbers in each pattern.

4 ☐ 10 13 16 ☐ 22

State the rule. _____

14 25 36 47 58 ☐ 80 ☐

State the rule. _____

2 8 5 11 8 ☐ ☐ ☐

State the rule. _____

☐ 9 11 33 35 105 107 ☐

State the rule. _____

Name _____

More Number Patterns

Solve each of the number patterns. Then tell the rule the pattern follows.

50   5   100   10   200 _____ _____   400   40 _____ _____

Rule: _____

6   10   14   7   11   15   8 _____ _____ _____

Rule: _____

987   876   765   654 _____ _____ _____

Rule: _____

2   4   16   256 _____

Rule: _____

Create your own pattern. Write the rule below it.

Thinking Skills, Grades 5–6 • EMC 5303

Earning a Living in 1860

Logical Thinking, 21, Deductive Reasoning

Introducing the Skill

1. Review the pronunciation of the vocabulary words used in this lesson. Do not give definitions.

2. Remind students to mark the grid when they have information that eliminates or affirms the meaning of a word. Whenever they write a *yes*, there should be an *X* in all the other boxes in that row and column.

Using the Chart and Activity Page

1. Show Chart 21.

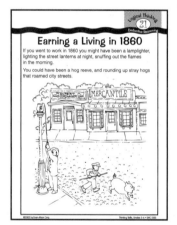

2. Distribute the activity page, *Earning a Living in 1860,* found on page 92.

3. Students read the clues about the jobs in 1860. They will identify the true statement and then fill in the grid.

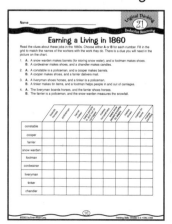

Extending the Skill

Have students select one of the jobs listed on the chart and student page. After learning more about the job, they might write about a typical day in the life of the worker. Have them tell whether they would like to do the job.

Reasoning Plan for Solving the Matrix

- The clue in the picture is the "Cordwainer" sign in the window where shoes are displayed. This makes statement 1B correct.

- Mark *yes* in the boxes for cordwainer/makes shoes and chandler/makes candles.

- If a cordwainer makes shoes, then 2B is not true. Therefore 2A is true. Write *yes* for constable/policeman and cooper/barrel maker.

- Now you know that 4B can't be true (if a constable is a policeman, a farrier is not a policeman), so 4A is true. Write *yes* for liveryman/boards horses and farrier/makes horseshoes.

- Now you know that 3A is not true, so 3B is true. Write *yes* for tinker/makes tin items and footman/helps people in and out of carriages.

- After matching these jobs, the only box remaining tells us that a snow warden keeps snow packed smoothly for sleighs.

Drag *X* or *yes* into each square to complete the matrix.

©2002 by Evan-Moor Corp.

Thinking Skills, Grades 5–6 • EMC 5303

Earning a Living in 1860

If you went to work in 1860 you might have been a lamplighter, lighting the street lanterns at night, and snuffing out the flames in the morning.

You could have been a hog reeve, rounding up stray hogs that roamed city streets.

Name _____

Earning a Living in 1860

Read the clues about these jobs in the 1860s. Choose either **A** or **B** for each number. Fill in the grid to match the names of the workers with the work they do. There is a clue you will need in the picture on the chart.

1. **A.** A snow warden makes barrels (for storing snow water), and a footman makes shoes.
   B. A cordwainer makes shoes, and a chandler makes candles.

2. **A.** A constable is a policeman, and a cooper makes barrels.
   B. A cooper makes shoes, and a farrier delivers mail.

3. **A.** A liveryman shoes horses, and a tinker is a policeman.
   B. A tinker makes tin items, and a footman helps people in and out of carriages.

4. **A.** The liveryman boards horses, and the farrier shoes horses.
   B. The farrier is a policeman, and the snow warden measures the snowfall.

	boards horses	policeman	barrel maker	helps people in and out of carriages	makes horseshoes	keeps snow packed smoothly for sleighs	makes shoes	makes tin items	makes candles
constable									
cooper									
farrier									
snow warden									
footman									
cordwainer									
liveryman									
tinker									
chandler									

Thinking Skills, Grades 5–6 • EMC 5303

The Quiet Quilters

Introducing the Skill

Review the strategies for solving table logic problems.

- Read all of the clues before beginning.

- Note what possibilities cannot exist to help you know what possibilities do exist. *For example, knowing that Essie cannot have the last names Ecker or Eaton will help determine what Essie's last name is.*

- The position of the chairs around the table is not important. The order of the quilters in the chairs is important.

Using the Chart and Activity Page

1. Show Chart 22.

2. Students read the clues about the quilters' names and their relative positions around the table. Then they write the names on the correct chairs.

3. Distribute the activity page, *At the Table,* found on page 95.

4. Have students look at the illustrated quilt pattern representing the quilt that the quilters are making. Read the descriptions of the four different quilts and name the quilt pictured.

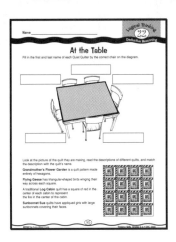

Extending the Skill

Have students research, draw, and describe additional quilt patterns.

Drag a first and last name into each box to show where the quilters sit.

Thinking Skills, Grades 5–6 • EMC 5303

The Quiet Quilters

The Quiet Quilters meet every Tuesday afternoon at the Patchwork Palace. They always sit in the same places as they quilt. Esther, Wilma, Rose, Essie, and Roxanne have the last names Eaton, Wood, Rich, Ecker, and Ross (but not in that order).

Read the clues and then write the first and last name of each Quiet Quilter by the correct chair.

Clues:

1. No quilters' last name begins with the same letter as her first name.

2. The quilter with the last name of Ecker sits to the right of the quilter with the last name of Eaton.

3. Rose's last name is not Eaton.

4. Wilma sits between Essie and Esther.

5. The quilter with the last name of Rich sits next to Roxanne.

6. Esther's last name is not Wood.

At the Table

Fill in the first and last name of each Quiet Quilter by the correct chair on the diagram.

Look at the picture of the quilt they are making, read the descriptions of four different quilts, and match the description with the quilt's pattern.

Grandmother's Flower Garden is a quilt pattern made entirely of hexagons.

Flying Geese has triangular-shaped birds winging their way across each square.

A traditional **Log Cabin** quilt has a square of red in the center of each "cabin" to represent the fire in the center of the cabin.

Sunbonnet Sue quilts have appliqued girls with large sunbonnets covering their faces.

Quilt pattern: _____

In Days Gone By

Introducing the Skill

1. Show students several pictures of different types of fish swimming in water.

2. Ask them to make a general statement about the fish. Answers will vary, but they should say something like *"fish need water"* or *"fish swim in water."* Explain that making a general or overall statement after observing specific examples is called **generalizing**.

Using the Chart and Activity Page

1. Show Chart 23.

2. Give students time to write several generalizations that they can make after looking at the page.

3. Distribute the activity page, *Making Generalizations,* found on page 98.

4. Have students write a generalization after reading the three bits of information.

5. Share the generalizations.

Extending the Skill

Have students study one part of Native American culture, such as games that Native American children played. Students note specific information and then write a generalization about the topic.

Click in the text box to keyboard students' responses.

Thinking Skills, Grades 5–6 • EMC 5303

In Days Gone By

Look at these pictures of Native Americans. They lived in different parts of America. Write a caption that applies to all of the pictures.

Making Generalizations

Read the following facts about the traditional dress of Native Americans. Write several sentences to generalize the similarities and differences that you note.

- Native American children living in warm desert areas wore practically nothing. Native American children living in the cold north wore layers of hides and furs.

- Native Americans who had to spend all their time looking for food didn't have much time for making fancy or beautiful things to wear. Those who had plenty of food had the time to create intricate jewelry and clothing with elaborate decorations made from quills, shells, beads, paints, and embroidery.

- Tribes in the central plains area usually wore clothing made of hides. Those living in the warm grasslands of California wove their simple clothing from grass and went barefoot.

_____

_____

_____

_____

_____

_____

_____

Wildflower Harvest

Introducing the Skill

1. Present several attention-getting newspaper headlines.

2. Discuss how the headlines invite the reader to read the article. Explain that the headline of a newspaper story is written to attract the reader's attention. It must be interesting while it generalizes the information in the newspaper article.

Using the Chart and Activity Page

1. Show Chart 24.

2. Read the information on the chart.

3. Have students write a headline. Remind them that the headline should attract the reader's attention and generalize the information on the chart.

4. Share students' headlines.

5. Distribute the activity page, *Useful Plants,* on page 101. Students will read this additional information about plants. They will then match the name of the plants with the plants' descriptions.

Extending the Skill

After students work with the chart and the student page, they may classify the plants on the pages. The answers will vary, but medicinal and edible plants could be classified by using a Venn diagram.

Click in the text box to keyboard students' responses.

Thinking Skills, Grades 5–6 • EMC 5303

Wildflower Harvest

Write one statement about these wild plants that could be used as an eye-catching newspaper headline.

Bloodroot is a spring-flowering plant. It is used in some toothpastes and mouthwashes to control plaque.

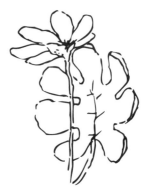

The leaves of the borage plant are rich in vitamin C. They taste like cucumbers. They are served in salads.

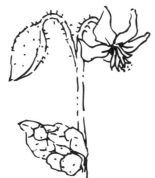

The foxglove is poisonous, but it has medical uses. Digitalis, an important heart medicine, comes from the plant.

The Hercules club has thorny trunks and branches. The bark and foliage numb the mouth and relieve a toothache when chewed.

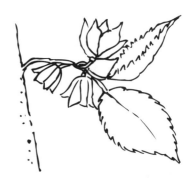

Useful Plants

Match the sentences about the different plants with the names of the plants. Write the number for the sentences that describe the plant.

wintergreen _____   celandine _____   chamomile _____

eucalyptus _____   witch hazel _____

1. It's a member of the poppy family. Orange sap from the stem has been used as an eyewash.
   Clue: Even though a part of the word means "to eat," it's not a food.

2. Strong-smelling leaves from this Australian tree produce an oil that is used in perfumes, deodorants, and medicines.
   Clue: The word begins with "you."

3. A tea is made from the dried flowers of this plant. It has been used for upset stomachs and sleeplessness.
   Clue: Lots of moms have served this tea when their children were sick.

4. A lotion is made from the bark and leaves of this shrub.
   Clue: Eyes can be brown, blue, green, or...?

5. Oil from this plant is used to flavor gum and candy. It is added to creams to sooth sore muscles.
   Clue: It's a very seasonal word.

     Thinking Skills, Grades 5–6 • EMC 5303

A Serious Discussion

Introducing the Skill

This lesson reviews three of the thinking skill processes students have used before. They will be asked to solve a table logic problem, brainstorm and list problems that might face a high school student body, and suggest solutions for solving one of the problems.

Using the Chart and Activity Page

1. Show Chart 25.

2. Distribute the activity page, *Seating Chart*, found on page 104.

3. Students begin by placing the student leaders in position around the table. Read the clues about their positions at the table and then solve the puzzle.

4. Brainstorm problems that might really be solved in sessions like the one in *A Serious Discussion.* List the problems on the chalkboard or a chart.

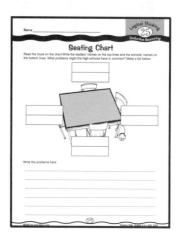

Extending the Skill

Have students select one of the problems listed on the chalkboard or chart and develop possible solutions.

Drag each person's name and school to the correct position around the table.

Thinking Skills, Grades 5–6 • EMC 5303

A Serious Discussion

The student body presidents from four high schools decide to get together and talk about their schools' problems. Find out which school each leader is from and where they each sit at the meeting.

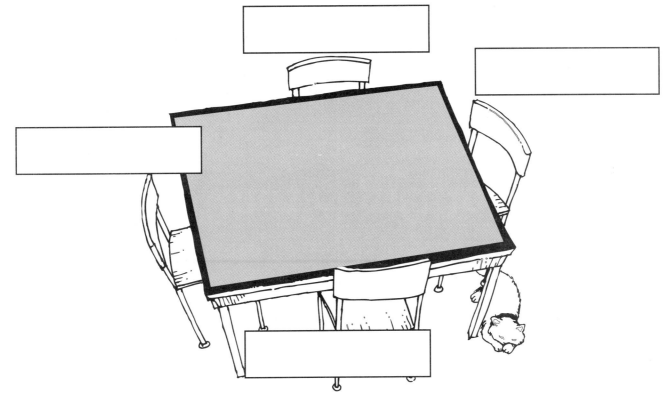

Clues:

1. Frederick Hill does not remember ever meeting Francesca Tito. They do not sit next to each other.

2. The leader from North High and the leader from East Memorial High are very good friends, but they do not sit next to each other.

3. The leader from Centennial High wants to know Sophie Silver better, so he sits next to her.

4. The leader from Uptown High sits next to Allen Sang.

5. The leader from North High sits to the right of Francesca Tito.

6. The leader from East Memorial High sits across from Allen Sang, but the leader from Centennial High does not sit next to Francesca.

Seating Chart

Read the clues on the chart. Write the leaders' names on the top lines and the schools' names on the bottom lines. What problems might the high schools have in common? Make a list below.

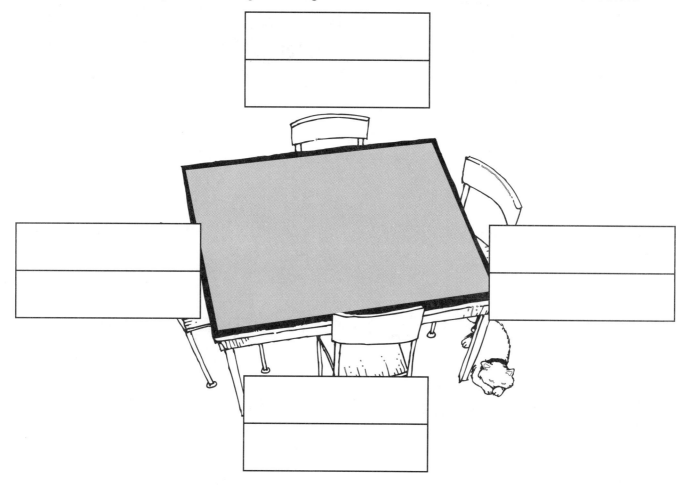

Write the problems here:

_____

_____

_____

_____

_____

_____

Thinking Skills, Grades 5–6 • EMC 5303

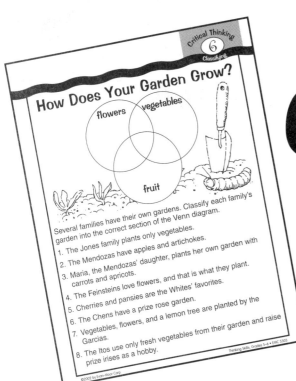

How Does Your Garden Grow?

flowers   vegetables

fruit

Several families have their own gardens. Classify each family's garden into the correct section of the Venn diagram.

1. The Jones family plants only vegetables.

2. The Mendozas have apples and artichokes.

3. Maria, the Mendozas' daughter, plants her own garden with carrots and apricots.

4. The Feinsteins love flowers, and that is what they plant.

5. Cherries and pansies are the Whites' favorites.

6. The Chens have a prize rose garden.

7. Vegetables, flowers, and a lemon tree are planted by the Garcias.

8. The Itos use only fresh vegetables from their garden and raise prize irises as a hobby.

Thinking Skills, Grades 5–6 • EMC 5303

©2002 by Evan-Moor Corp.

Critical Thinking

Thinking Skills, Grades 5–6 • EMC 5303

Let's Get Organized!

Introducing the Skill

1. Ask students to make a list of things that they keep in their desks.

2. Have them explain if the items are arranged in any particular way.

   Are writing materials kept in a box?

   Are homework papers kept in a folder?

   Are books kept to one side?

Using the Chart and Activity Page

1. Show Chart 1.

2. Distribute the activity page, *Let's Get Organized!,* found on page 108. Students will cut out the pictures on this page and sort them into different categories.

3. Explain the task given on the chart. Set a minimum number of possible arrangements that each student should create.

4. Students arrange the closet contents in several different ways, keeping a written record of the different categories they use.

5. Share student work.

Extending the Skill

Have students develop a new organizational plan for the coat rack or art-supply cupboard by classifying the materials and organizing materials by categories.

Click and drag objects into groups.

Thinking Skills, Grades 5–6 • EMC 5303

Let's Get Organized!

John and Sam are twins who share a bedroom. They are organizing the shelves in their closet so it will be easier to find what they need. They decided to group items that are related and make labels for the shelves. How many different ways can you classify all the objects on the chart? Each group of objects must have at least two items.

Name _____

Let's Get Organized!

John and Sam's belongings are pictured below. Cut out the pictures. Arrange all 18 pictures into groups. On a sheet of paper, write a name for each group and list the objects in the group.

©2002 by Evan-Moor Corp.

Thinking Skills, Grades 5–6 • EMC 5303

It's on the Map

Introducing the Skill

Reading a map is one way to analyze information. While students may see this activity as basic map reading, they are asked to make inferences from the information on the map and in the questions that require critical thinking. The activity then becomes a good way to show a connection between learning to use thinking skills such as analyzing and doing everyday things like reading a map.

Using the Chart and Activity Page

1. Show Chart 2.

2. Distribute the activity page, *It's on the Map,* found on page 111.

3. Students read and answer the questions on the activity page.

Extending the Skill

1. Have students invent a map of an imaginary place. They should mark cities, mountains, lakes, rivers, and other landmarks. Each map should have a key with colors and shapes as symbols.

2. Each mapmaker creates a set of questions about the map and challenges classmates to answer the questions.

Click on a symbol in the key. Corresponding locations on the map will change color.

Thinking Skills, Grades 5–6 • EMC 5303

It's on the Map

Use the map to answer the questions on your worksheet.

Oregon

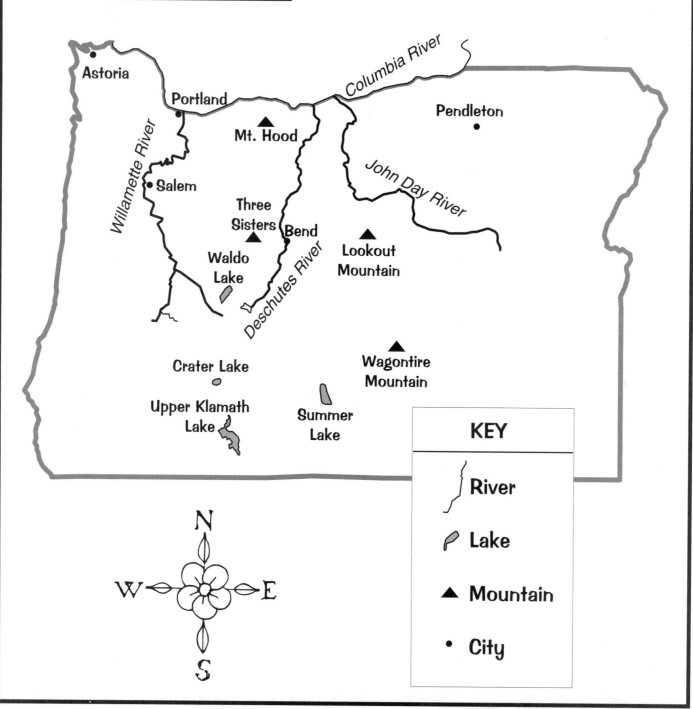

Astoria

Portland

Columbia River

Pendleton

Mt. Hood

Willamette River

Salem

John Day River

Three
Sisters

Bend

Lookout
Mountain

Waldo
Lake

Deschutes River

Crater Lake

Wagontire
Mountain

Upper Klamath
Lake

Summer
Lake

KEY

River

Lake

▲ Mountain

• City

N

W   E

S

It's on the Map

Use the map of Oregon on Chart 2 to answer the following questions.

_____ 1. Which river was named after an early settler?

_____ 2. Which lake was formed when the top of a volcano blew off?

_____ 3. Which mountain might you see if you cruised east from Portland on the Columbia River?

_____ 4. If you rafted the Deschutes from Bend to the Columbia, in which direction would you be traveling?

_____ 5. Are the cities shown in the northern or southern part of the state?

_____ 6. Which mountain is east of Bend?

_____ 7. One of the cities shown is a shipping center for oceangoing vessels. Which one? (Hint: Its name will tell you.)

_____ 8. The state of Washington lies to the north of Oregon. Name the river that forms part of the boundary between the two states.

_____ 9. The largest lake is actually a reservoir formed by a dam. What is the name of the lake?

Bonus: How do you think the city of Bend got its name?

_____

Thinking Skills, Grades 5–6 • EMC 5303

Endangered Mammals of the Sea

Introducing the Skill

When the classification table on the activity page is introduced, explain that the sizes of students in the classroom vary and so do sizes of a particular type of animal. *(For example, not all seals weigh 600 pounds.)* Students should work with the numbers on page 114, however, to classify the marine mammals.

Using the Chart and Activity Page

1. Show Chart 3.

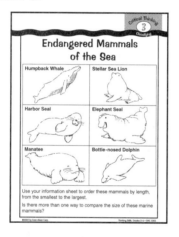

2. Distribute the activity page, *Marine Mammal Facts,* found on page 114.

3. Students use the information on the activity page to order the mammals from shortest to longest.

4. Then have students think of other possible ways to compare and order the size of marine mammals *(for example, by weight).*

5. The mammals on the chart can also be grouped (not ordered) into different categories. Have your students brainstorm possible groups *(for example, toothed and toothless)* and organize the mammals into those groups.

Extending the Skill

1. Have each student choose a marine mammal to add to a class chart.

2. Using reference materials, the student provides the information needed to classify the mammal with the others.

Click in the small boxes and keyboard a number to order the mammals.

Thinking Skills, Grades 5–6 • EMC 5303

Endangered Mammals of the Sea

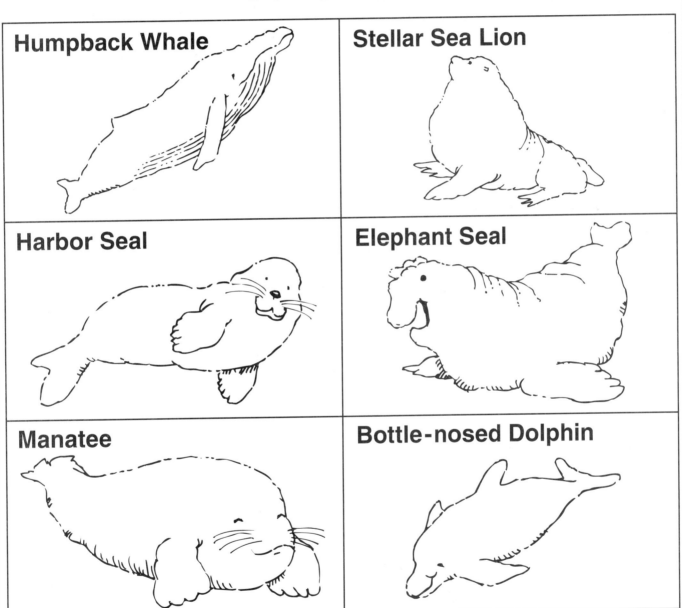

Humpback Whale

Stellar Sea Lion

Harbor Seal

Elephant Seal

Manatee

Bottle-nosed Dolphin

Use your information sheet to order these mammals by length, from the smallest to the largest.

Is there more than one way to compare the size of these marine mammals?

Name _____

Marine Mammal Facts

Read about each of the following mammals. Use the information to group the mammals in as many ways as you can. Write your groupings on a separate sheet of paper.

Mammal Name	Size	Habitat	Special Features
Humpback Whale	• 57 feet long (17.5 m) • 10.5 tons (10,670 kg)	lives in the Atlantic and the north Pacific Oceans	• warm-blooded mammal • toothless • no external ears
Stellar Sea Lion	• 12 feet (3.5 m) • 2,300 pounds (1,043 kg)	lives on the northern Pacific coast	• have small ears • walk on their four limbs • warm-blooded mammal • pointed teeth
Harbor Seal	• up to 5.5 feet (1.7 m) • 550 pounds (250 kg)	lives in the waters on the north Atlantic and Pacific coasts	• find their food in the sea • breed on land • cannot walk on land—inch themselves forward • no external ears
Manatee	• 13 feet (4.5 m) • up to 2,000 pounds (900 kg)	lives in southeastern U.S., Caribbean Sea, northern South America	• relative of the elephant • slow moving—swim at about 5 miles per hour • can stay underwater for nearly 15 minutes when feeding
Elephant Seal	• female – up to 10 feet (3 m) and 2,000 pounds (900 kg) • male – up to 16 feet (5 m) to 5,500 pounds (2,500 kg)	lives on the Pacific coasts of North and South America; Antarctica	• thick layers of blubber • was favorite target of seal hunters • nose resembles the trunk of an elephant
Bottle-nosed Dolphin	• up to 12 feet (3.7 m) • up to 1,500 pounds (694 kg)	lives in temperate and warm waters worldwide	• pointed teeth in both jaws • bulging forehead • beaklike snout • no external ears

Thinking Skills, Grades 5–6 • EMC 5303

Where Do They Live?

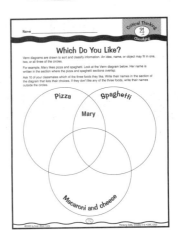

Introducing the Skill

Depending on the experience of your group, you may choose to name the additional four sections of the Venn diagram as a class or as an individual activity. On the chart, students will simply interpret the information that is given. When they do the activity page, they will be classifying information that they gather.

Using the Chart and Activity Page

1. Show Chart 4.

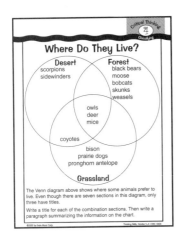

2. Have students write a title for each section of the Venn diagram. Then students write a paragraph summarizing the information on the chart.

3. Distribute the activity page, *Which Do You Like?*, found on page 117.

4. Have students interview 10 classmates to complete the diagram.

5. Provide time for students to share the completed diagrams. Ask them to explain what information they learned.

Extending the Skill

1. List three games or sports that students like to play.

2. Have students draw Venn diagrams and label them for the three sports.

3. Students then interview classmates and/or students in other classes, and write their names in the appropriate sections on the chart.

Click in the sections of the Venn diagram to keyboard titles of the combination sections. Then keyboard the summary in the large text box.

Thinking Skills, Grades 5–6 • EMC 5303

Where Do They Live?

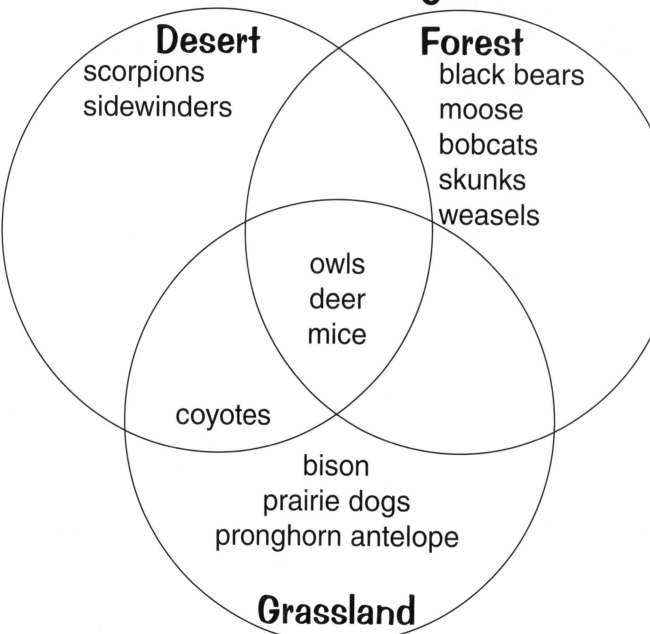

Desert
scorpions
sidewinders

Forest
black bears
moose
bobcats
skunks
weasels

owls
deer
mice

coyotes

bison
prairie dogs
pronghorn antelope

Grassland

The Venn diagram above shows where some animals prefer to live. Even though there are seven sections in this diagram, only three have titles.

Write a title for each of the combination sections. Then write a paragraph summarizing the information on the chart.

Which Do You Like?

Venn diagrams are drawn to sort and classify information. An idea, name, or object may fit in one, two, or all three of the circles.

For example, Mary likes pizza and spaghetti. Look at the Venn diagram below. Her name is written in the section where the pizza and spaghetti sections overlap.

Ask 10 of your classmates which of the three foods they like. Write their names in the section of the diagram that lists their choices. If they don't like any of the three foods, write their names outside the circles.

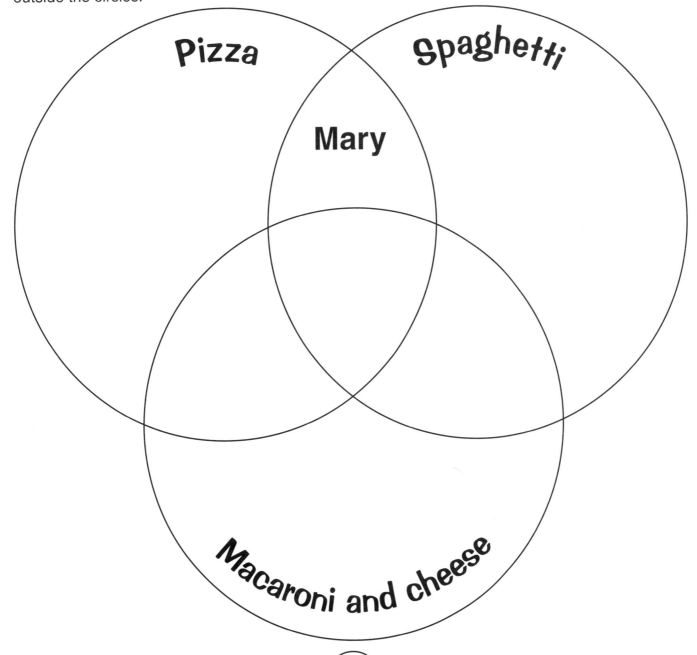

©2002 by Evan-Moor Corp.

Thinking Skills, Grades 5–6 • EMC 5303

Soft? White? Furry?

Introducing the Skill

It is likely that your students will have had previous experience with Venn diagrams. If you feel they need more practice identifying the categories and placing items in the categories, provide concrete experiences before doing the chart and worksheet. Create three overlapping circles on the floor with ropes or yarn. Use students as the objects to classify. For example, label circles:

Boys
Students on soccer teams
Bike riders

or

Students with glasses
Students wearing jeans
Students with short hair

or

Students wearing sweatshirts
Students with high-tops
Students with watches

Using the Chart and Activity Page

1. Show Chart 5.

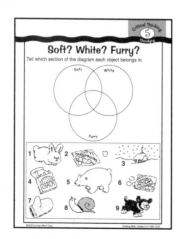

2. Have students label the intersecting sections of the diagram.

3. As a class, place each of the numbered objects into the diagram or beside the diagram.

4. Discuss the reasons that students have classified the objects the way that they have. Students may have good reasons for classifying objects differently.

5. Distribute the activity page, *Organizing Information,* found on page 120.

6. Students organize the information at the top of the page, using the information on the Venn diagram.

7. Ask students to explain how organizing information like this could be valuable in reporting research.

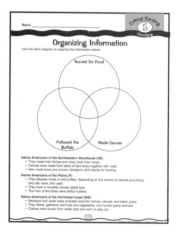

Extending the Skill

Have students use a Venn diagram as a graphic organizer for a writing assignment.

CD Tips

Drag the pictures into the appropriate sections of the diagram.

Thinking Skills, Grades 5–6 • EMC 5303

Soft? White? Furry?

Tell which section of the diagram each object belongs in.

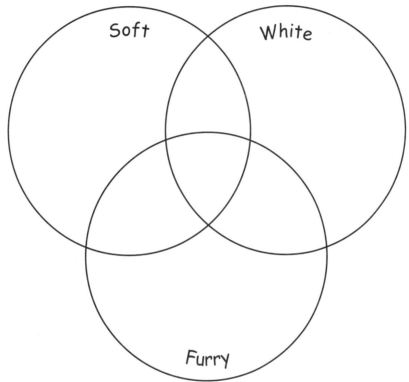

Soft   White

Furry

1

2   MARSHMALLOWS

3

4   CHALK

5

6   COTTON BALLS

7

8

9

Name _____

Organizing Information

Use the Venn diagram to organize the information below.

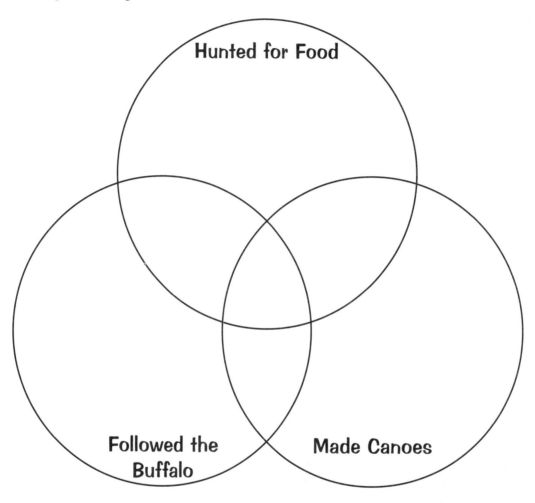

Hunted for Food

Followed the Buffalo

Made Canoes

Native Americans of the Northeastern Woodlands (NE)
- They made their homes and many tools from wood.
- Canoes were made from slabs of bark laced together with roots.
- Men made bows and arrows, blowguns, and snares for hunting.

Native Americans of the Plains (P)
- They followed herds of wild buffalo, depending on this animal for almost everything they ate, wore, and used.
- They lived in movable homes called tipis.
- The men of the tribes were skillful hunters.

Native Americans of the Northwest Coast (NW)
- Redwood and cedar trees provided wood for homes, canoes, and totem poles.
- They fished, gathered wild fruits and vegetables, and hunted game animals.
- Clothes were woven from cedar bark and worn to stay dry.

120

How Does Your Garden Grow?

Introducing the Skill

Students will use prior knowledge to help them interpret the information given and place the gardens into the correct sections of the Venn diagram.

Using the Chart and Activity Page

1. Show Chart 6.

2. Read the information to identify the families and classify their gardens.

3. Students complete the activity page, *Insect Investigation,* on page 123. They will draw and label their own Venn diagrams and then complete them.

4. Provide time to discuss the attributes that students have chosen to use for classification.

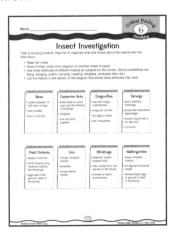

Extending the Skill

1. Brainstorm the attributes of a good book. Record the attributes on the chalkboard or overhead projector.

2. Each student chooses three of the attributes, then draws and labels a Venn diagram.

3. Use the Venn diagram to evaluate the books students have read.

Click in each section of the Venn diagram to add names.

Thinking Skills, Grades 5–6 • EMC 5303

How Does Your Garden Grow?

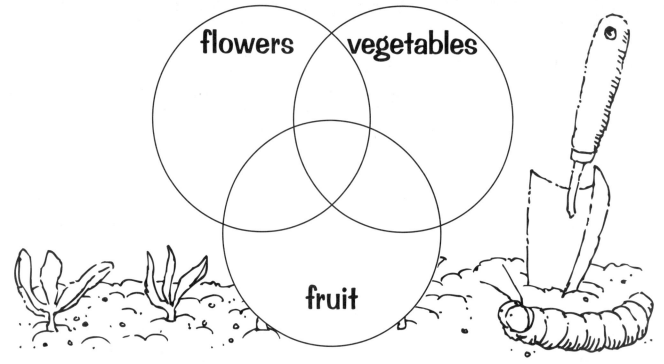

Several families have their own gardens. Classify each family's garden into the correct section of the Venn diagram.

1. The Jones family plants only vegetables.

2. The Mendozas have apples and artichokes.

3. Maria, the Mendozas' daughter, plants her own garden with carrots and apricots.

4. The Feinsteins love flowers, and that is what they plant.

5. Cherries and pansies are the Whites' favorites.

6. The Chens have a prize rose garden.

7. Vegetables, flowers, and a lemon tree are planted by the Garcias.

8. The Itos use only fresh vegetables from their garden and raise prize irises as a hobby.

Name _____

Insect Investigation

Yoko is studying insects. Help her to organize what she knows about the insects she has read about.

- Read her notes.
- Draw a three-circle Venn diagram on another sheet of paper.
- Use three attributes of different insects as subjects for the circles. (Some possibilities are flying, stinging, pollen-carrying, crawling, wingless, produces odor, etc.)
- List the insects in the section of the diagram that shows what attributes they have.

Bees
- "pollen baskets" of stiff hairs on legs
- hairy bodies
- live in colonies

Carpenter Ants
- build nests in wood, logs, and the timbers of buildings
- wingless
- live and work together

Dragonflies
- rest with wings outstretched
- wings do not fold
- lay eggs in water
- eat mosquitoes

Earwigs
- short, leathery forewings
- pincer-like abdominal appendage
- exude a liquid with a tar-like odor
- nocturnal

Field Crickets
- largely nocturnal
- shrill musical song made by rubbing the forewings
- eggs laid in the ground, hatch in the spring

Lice
- minute, wingless insects
- parasites
- young mature rapidly

Stinkbugs
- flattened, shield-shaped body
- odor comes from two glands on the thorax
- colored to match environment

Walkingsticks
- large, wingless insects
- all legs are the same length
- female drops eggs to ground to hatch in the spring

Thinking Skills, Grades 5–6 • EMC 5303

Wildflowers

Introducing the Skill

1. Display copies of wildflower books like the *Audubon Society Field Guide to North American Wildflowers* so that students are familiar with the variety and color of the flowers.

2. Show at least one example of each of the categories on the Venn diagram so that students will know what is meant by *five petals, many flowers on one stem,* and *bell- or trumpet-shaped flowers.*

Using the Chart and Activity Page

1. Show Chart 7.

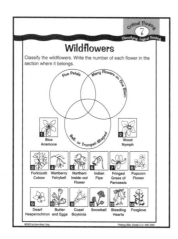

2. Solve the diagram as a group, or have students copy the Venn diagram circles and do the classifying independently.

3. Distribute the activity page, *Flower Patterns,* found on page 126.

4. Students cut out the pieces of the wheel and put the puzzle together.

5. Then have students identify the pattern in the design.

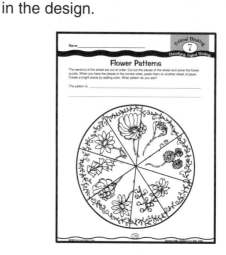

Extending the Skill

1. Have students look through wildflower books and add the names of other flowers to the diagram.

2. Student groups brainstorm different ways to classify flowers. Then they use reference materials to find out how scientists classify flowers.

Drag the number of each flower into the section where it belongs.

124

Wildflowers

Classify the wildflowers. Write the number of each flower in the section where it belongs.

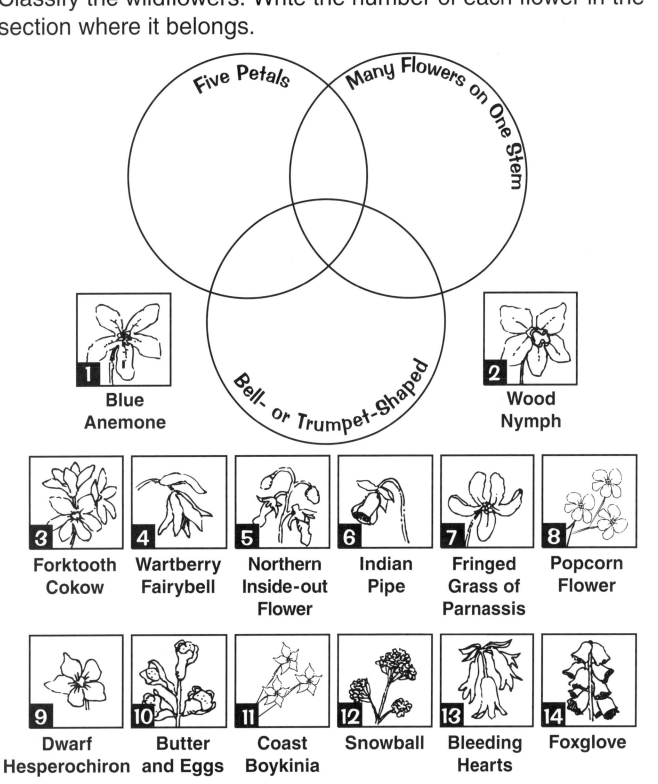

Five Petals

Many Flowers on One Stem

Bell- or Trumpet-Shaped

1 Blue Anemone

2 Wood Nymph

3 Forktooth Cokow

4 Wartberry Fairybell

5 Northern Inside-out Flower

6 Indian Pipe

7 Fringed Grass of Parnassis

8 Popcorn Flower

9 Dwarf Hesperochiron

10 Butter and Eggs

11 Coast Boykinia

12 Snowball

13 Bleeding Hearts

14 Foxglove

Flower Patterns

The sections of the wheel are out of order. Cut out the pieces of the wheel and solve the flower puzzle. When you have the pieces in the correct order, paste them on another sheet of paper. Create a bright scene by adding color. What pattern do you see?

The pattern is _____

_____

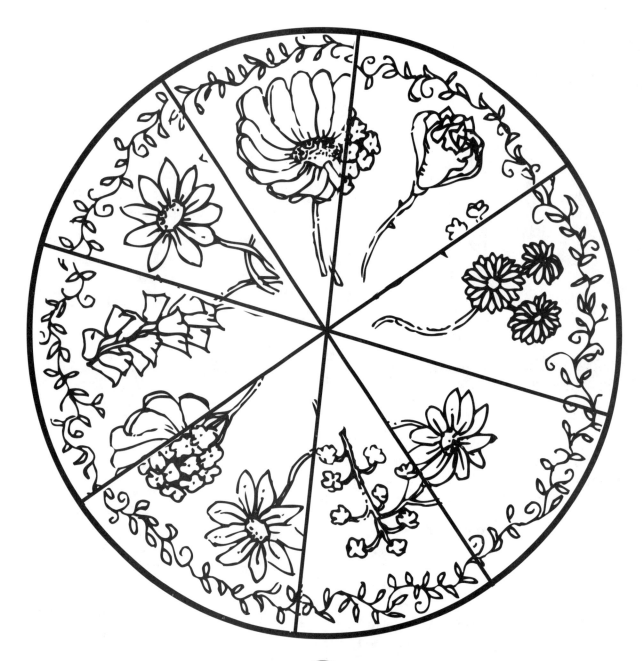

A Buggy Puzzle

Introducing the Skill

1. Have students describe their "favorite" bugs.

2. After several descriptions, ask students to list attributes that were common to the bugs described.

3. Explain that students will use the attributes to help distinguish between the bugs on the chart.

Using the Chart and Activity Page

1. Show Chart 8.

2. Distribute the activity page, *A Buggy Puzzle,* found on page 129.

3. Students identify and match the insects on the two charts to find the missing ones.

4. Discuss the strategies that students may have had for matching the insects and keeping track of their observations.

Extending the Skill

1. Prepare a tray of familiar classroom objects.

2. Have students look at the tray for a minute.

3. Remove or cover the tray. Secretly remove one object.

4. Have students determine the missing object.

Click on the insects as you match them to make them disappear.

Thinking Skills, Grades 5–6 • EMC 5303

A Buggy Puzzle

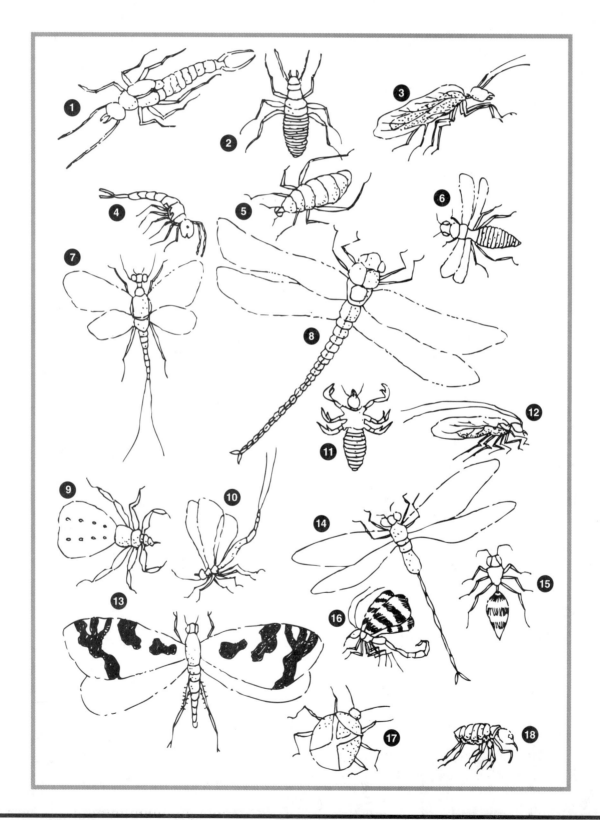

Name _____

A Buggy Puzzle

Bugs creep and fly about. All the bugs on this page were on Chart 8, but some of the bugs are missing. Can you tell which ones?

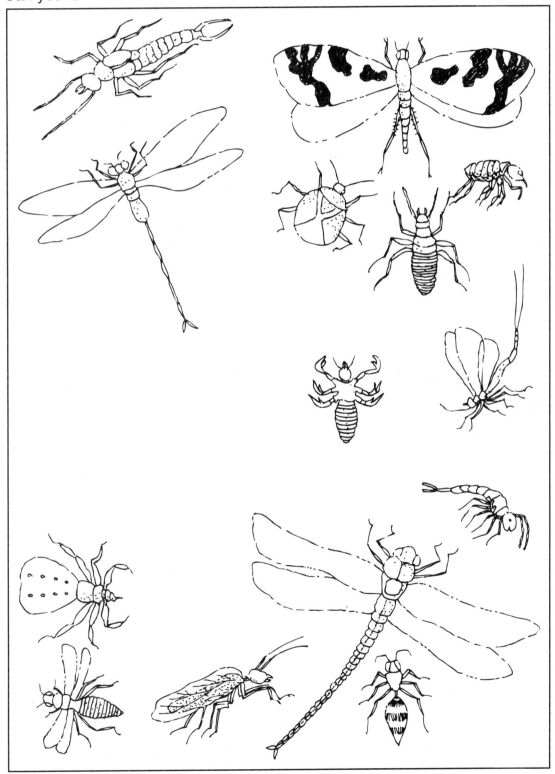

129

Mapping the Truth

Introducing the Skill

Students will draw from their prior knowledge to tell why the statements on the chart are untrue. They need to know:

- that high altitudes, even near the equator, are often cold at night, and

- that seasons are reversed in the Southern Hemisphere.

Using the Chart and Activity Page

1. Show Chart 9.

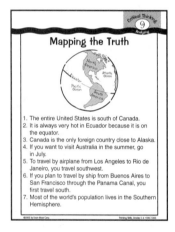

2. Distribute the world map on the activity page on page 132.

3. Students use the map to tell why the statements on the chart are untrue.

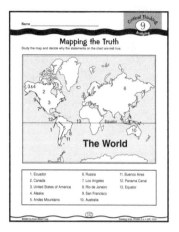

Extending the Skill

Have students write correct statements about each of the countries or regions mentioned on the chart.

Click on each statement to highlight it.

Mapping the Truth

1. The entire United States is south of Canada.
2. It is always very hot in Ecuador because it is on the equator.
3. Canada is the only foreign country close to Alaska.
4. If you want to visit Australia in the summer, go in July.
5. To travel by airplane from Los Angeles to Rio de Janeiro, you travel southwest.
6. If you plan to travel by ship from Buenos Aires to San Francisco through the Panama Canal, you first travel south.
7. Most of the world's population lives in the Southern Hemisphere.

Mapping the Truth

Study the map and decide why the statements on the chart are **not** true.

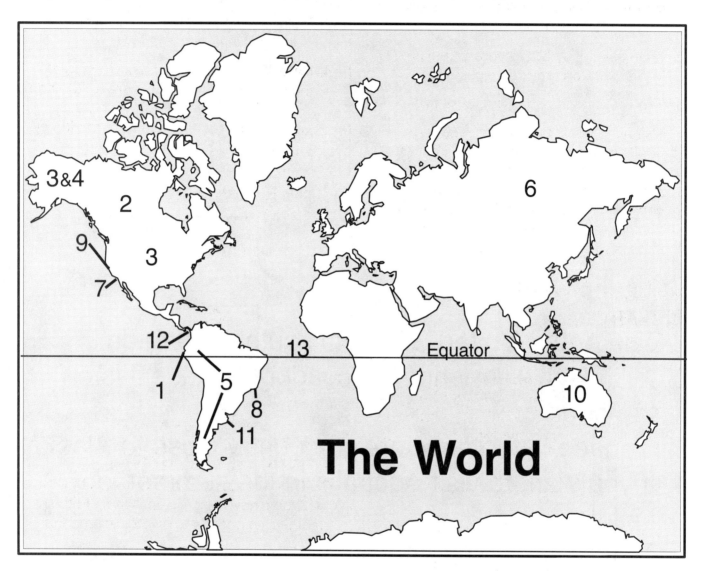

3&4

2

9

7

6

3

12

13   Equator

1

5

8

10

11

The World

1. Ecuador	6. Russia	11. Buenos Aires
2. Canada	7. Los Angeles	12. Panama Canal
3. United States of America	8. Rio de Janeiro	13. Equator
4. Alaska	9. San Francisco	
5. Andes Mountains	10. Australia	

Thinking Skills, Grades 5–6 • EMC 5303

Proverbially Speaking

Introducing the Skill

1. Ask students if they have ever spilled their milk. Discuss their feelings and what they did to "repair" the damage.

2. Then ask if they have ever had anyone tell them, "Don't cry over spilt milk."

3. Explain that the phrase is a **proverb**.

   A proverb can have a literal meaning—don't cry if you spill your milk—and an implied meaning—don't complain about something that has already happened and can't be changed. (If milk spills out of a container, it can't be put back in, so you might as well not cry over it.)

Using the Chart and Activity Page

1. Show Chart 10.

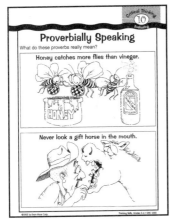

2. Discuss the two proverbs on the chart. The illustrations show the literal meanings. Have students provide the implied meanings.

   Honey catches more flies than vinegar. (Politeness and gentle words get better results than harsh words and demands.)

   Never look a gift horse in the mouth. (Don't find fault with something that you get for nothing.)

3. Distribute the activity page, *Proverbially Speaking,* found on page 135.

4. Have students work in pairs to complete the worksheet. Two heads are better than one! Students are asked not only to interpret the proverbs, but also to identify another proverb that has an opposite or similar meaning.

5. Share student work.

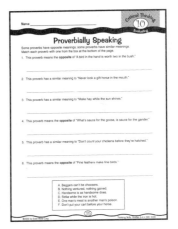

Extending the Skill

Challenge students to find proverbs that have meanings they think are applicable to their lives. Create posters to display around the school.

Click in the text boxes to keyboard students' responses.

Thinking Skills, Grades 5–6 • EMC 5303

Proverbially Speaking

What do these proverbs really mean?

Honey catches more flies than vinegar.

Never look a gift horse in the mouth.

Proverbially Speaking

Some proverbs have opposite meanings; some proverbs have similar meanings.
Match each proverb with one from the box at the bottom of the page.

1. This proverb means the **opposite** of "A bird in the hand is worth two in the bush."

   _____

2. This proverb has a similar meaning to "Never look a gift horse in the mouth."

   _____

3. This proverb has a similar meaning to "Make hay while the sun shines."

   _____

4. This proverb means the **opposite** of "What's sauce for the goose, is sauce for the gander."

   _____

5. This proverb has a similar meaning to "Don't count your chickens before they're hatched."

   _____

6. This proverb means the **opposite** of "Fine feathers make fine birds."

   _____

A. Beggars can't be choosers.
B. Nothing ventured, nothing gained.
C. Handsome is as handsome does.
D. Strike while the iron is hot.
E. One man's meat is another man's poison.
F. Don't put your cart before your horse.

135

Getting Specific

Introducing the Skill

Categorizing and ordering words according to specific criteria gives students practice in thinking in an organized manner.

1. Place the following objects on a table:

   a math book
   a social studies book
   a library book
   a globe
   a reading book
   a lunchroom tray

2. Ask students to suggest a name for all the objects on the table. *(things that you find in a school)*

3. Then ask students if they can group three things in another category. *(The four books could be grouped together.)*

4. Write the three groups that the math book belongs to in order from general to specific.

   school things
   books
   math book

Using the Chart and Activity Page

1. Show Chart 11.

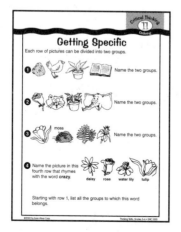

2. Ask students to identify the pictures in the first three rows and to classify the things into two groups.

3. Record the classifications for each row.

4. Name the flower in the fourth row that rhymes with *crazy. (daisy)*

5. Look at the categories for the first three rows. List the groups that the daisy belongs to in order from general to specific.

6. Distribute the activity page, *Getting Specific,* found on page 138.

7. Students practice ordering things from general to specific.

Extending the Skill

1. If your group seems ready, reverse the process and practice categorizing and ordering from specific to general. Ask a female student volunteer to come to the front of the room. Have her state her name. *(That is the most specific group.)*

2. Then ask students to suggest a name for the next most specific group to which she belongs. *(This might be "girls.")*

3. Continue, moving to a less specific group with each category. *(The next most specific group might be "student.")* The completed sequence might look like this:

   Mary
   girl
   student
   human being
   living creature

CD Tips

Click and drag the letter *A* or *B* beside each picture to designate its group. Then click in the corresponding text boxes to record students' responses.

Thinking Skills, Grades 5–6 • EMC 5303

Getting Specific

Each row of pictures can be divided into two groups.

1  Name the two groups.

2  Name the two groups.

3 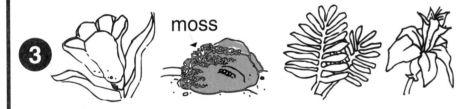 Name the two groups.

moss

4 Name the picture in this fourth row that rhymes with the word **crazy**.

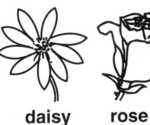

daisy   rose   water lily   tulip

Starting with row 1, list all the groups to which this word belongs.

Getting Specific

Write each list of words below in order, from general to specific.

1. rose, flower, plant, tea rose

_____

2. insect, living thing, bumblebee, animal

_____

3. head, eye, body part, iris

_____

4. toes, leg, body part, foot, nails

_____

5. tornado, weather system, storm

_____

Fill in the missing category that completes each word list in order, from general to specific.

6. animal _____ beagle

7. _____ vegetable broccoli

8. animal reptile _____

Write a three-word category list that moves from general to specific.

9. _____

Answer Key

Creative Thinking

Chart 1
Answers will vary.

Activity Page 7
Used in conjunction with the activity page.

Chart 2
There are 34,650 possible arrangements. You might want to set a goal for the number of arrangements that is reasonable for your group.

Activity Page 10
Used in conjunction with the chart.

Chart 3
snow, snow, snow, sunshine

Activity Page 13
kinds of leaves: 4; number of leaves: 8

Chart 4
2 left—sheep; 4 right—sheep; 1 left—pig;
3 left—sheep; 2 right—goose; 3 left—pig;
1 right—sheep; 2 left—goose; 1 right—pig

Activity Page 16
Students' game boards will vary.

Chart 5
Section 1—dog
Section 2—dog (feet facing left), flower
Section 3—bird (upside down), fish

Activity Page 19
bottom, bottom, bottom,
back, back, left

Chart 6
Responses will vary.

Activity Page 22
Responses will vary.

Chart 7

1	8	4
6	9	3
2	7	5

Activity Page 25

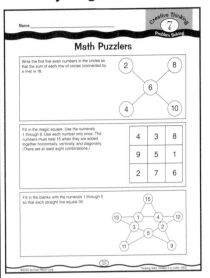

Chart 8
Used in conjunction with the activity page.

Activity Page 28

Logical Thinking

Chart 1
vain

Activity Page 32
clever

Chart 2

Fly has the place of honor in Seat 1 in the skydome. His great eyes make him a terrific lookout. He can buzz around all he wants.

Seat 2—Carrot
Seat 3—Spider
Seat 4—Rabbit
Seat 5—Human
Seat 6—Guinea Pig
Seat 7—Bird

Activity Page 35

A—zebras
B—rhinoceros
C—lions
D—hippos
E—elephants
F—sea lions

Chart 3

farmer

Activity Page 38

1. floor
2. clock
3. flock
4. cabbage
5. mice
6. Mexico
7. light
8. little

Chart 4

1. cockpit
2. house
3. camera
4. golf tee
5. bird
6. leash

Activity Page 41

1. page : book :: bone : body
2. dime : money :: German : language
3. blood : vein :: water : aqueduct
Original analogies will vary.

Chart 5

fluffy : sleek
sleeping : awake
big : little
quiet : loud
short tail : long tail
sweet : mean
long hair : short hair

Activity Page 44

Answers will vary.

Chart 6

The correct order is giraffes, lions, monkeys, and zebras.

Activity Page 47

The unnecessary facts are 7 and 10.
The shirt and shorts belong to Sean.
The jeans and jacket belong to Terry.
The dress belongs to Sammy.

The shoes and socks belong to Bobbie.

Chart 7

Used in conjunction with the activity page.

Activity Page 50

Javiar got off at D & Main.
Maria and Carlos got off at F & Main.
Liz and Edward got off at G & Main.
Sam, Alicia, Muhammad, and Darice got off at G & Central.
Emil got off at G & Broadway.

Chart 8

A—Douglas fir
B—American elm
C—one-leaf piñon
D—red maple
E—Sabal palmetto
F—live oak
G—redwood

Activity Page 53

Oregon—Douglas fir
Massachusetts, Nebraska, North Dakota— American elm
Rhode Island—red maple
California—redwood
Florida, South Carolina—Sabal palmetto
Nevada—one-leaf piñon
Georgia—live oak

Chart 9

1. all girls like ice cream
2. all feline Persians are purring animals
3. all chickens have feathers
4. the sun is in the sky
5. no insects are apples

Activity Page 56

Therefore, some flowers have thorns.
Therefore, some furniture is made from wood.
Therefore, some insects are biting creatures.

Chart 10

valid, valid, invalid, invalid, invalid

Activity Page 59

1. invalid
2. valid
3. valid
4. invalid

Chart 11

1. Mt. St. Helens
2. Mt. Vesuvius
3. Krakatau
4. Mt. Pelee
5. Mt. Pinatubo

Activity Page 62

Krakatau—Indonesia
Mt. Vesuvius—Italy
Mt. St. Helens—United States
Mt. Pelee—Martinique
Mt. Pinatubo—Philippines

Chart 12

Used in conjunction with the activity page.

Activity Page 65

USA—lead
Canada—zinc
Chile—copper
Zaire—cobalt
Australia—aluminum
South Africa—gold

Chart 13

Used in conjunction with the activity page.

Activity Page 68

Name ____________________

Logical Thinking 13
Deductive Reasoning

Speedy Delivery

Label this matrix with information from the chart. Begin by listing the names of the delivery persons down the left side. As you read the clues, fill in the labels across the top. Each label will be a number of deliveries. Then reread the clues and fill in the grid.

	32	38	39	40	42	51	62
Quick Quincy	X	X	X	X	Yes	X	X
Swift Suzie	X	X	X	X	X	X	Yes
Fleet Florence	X	X	X	Yes	X	X	X
Nimble Ned	X	X	Yes	X	X	X	X
Agile Avery	Yes	X	X	X	X	X	X
Ready Rose	X	Yes	X	X	X	X	X
Prompt Peter	X	X	X	X	X	Yes	X

68

©2002 by Evan-Moor Corp. Thinking Skills, Grades 5–6 • EMC 5303

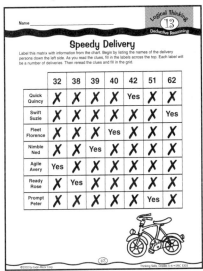

Chart 14

Used in conjunction with the activity page.

Activity Page 71

Name ____________________

Logical Thinking 14
Problem Solving

Holiday Shopping

Use the clues on Chart 14 to determine how much money each member of the Sutter family has saved for holiday shopping and where that person will go to shop.

When you know that a name and an amount of money or a name and a store do not go with each other, make an *X* under the money or store and across from the name. When you know that a name and an amount of money or a name and a store do go together, write ***yes*** in that box. You can then *X* that name and money or that name and store for all other possibilities.

	$25	$48	$72	$95	$120	$210	Impressive Imports	Larry's Lugage	Lots 'o Toys	Super Sports	Delightful Discounts	Something Jewelry
John	X	X	X	Yes	X	X	X	X	Yes	X	X	X
Carolyn	Yes	X	X	X	X	X	X	X	X	Yes	X	X
Michelle	X	X	Yes	X	X	X	X	Yes	X	X	X	X
Jeff	X	X	X	X	Yes	X	Yes	X	X	X	X	X
Julie	X	X	X	X	X	Yes	X	X	X	X	X	Yes
Emma	X	Yes	X	X	X	X	X	X	X	X	Yes	X

71

©2002 by Evan-Moor Corp. Thinking Skills, Grades 5–6 • EMC 5303

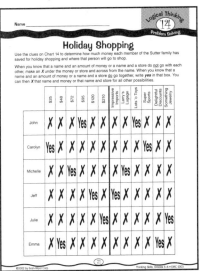

Chart 15

Used in conjunction with the activity page.

Activity Page 74

Name ____________________

Logical Thinking 15
Problem Solving

The Candy Store

74

©2002 by Evan-Moor Corp. Thinking Skills, Grades 5–6 • EMC 5303

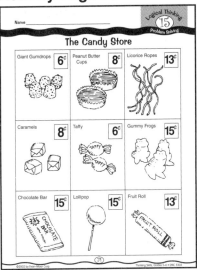

Chart 16

Used in conjunction with the activity page.

Activity Page 77

Name ____________________

Logical Thinking 16
Deductive Reasoning

The Collectors' Club Clues

Read the clues on the chart. Label the unlabeled rows and columns on the matrix. When you know that a boy and a color or a boy and a number of cards do not go with each other, make an *X* under the color or number of cards and across from the boy. When you know that a boy and color or a boy and number of cards do go together, write ***yes*** in that box.

	red	black	blue	green	315	720	1205	2403
Honus	X	X	X	Yes	X	X	Yes	X
Lou	Yes	X	X	X	Yes	X	X	X
Babe	X	X	Yes	X	X	X	X	Yes
Ty	X	Yes	X	X	X	Yes	X	X

77

©2002 by Evan-Moor Corp. Thinking Skills, Grades 5–6 • EMC 5303

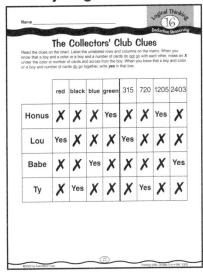

Chart 17

Used in conjunction with the activity page.

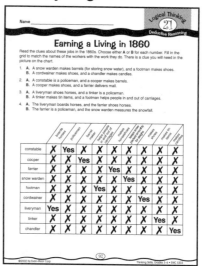

Chart 18
Used in conjunction with the activity page.

Activity Page 83
black fly—1; treehopper—2; dragonfly—1; cricket—3, 5; cockroach—4

Chart 19
Solutions will vary.

Activity Page 86
Information will vary.

Chart 20
4 [7] 10 13 16 [19] 22 (+3)

14 25 36 47 58 [69] 80 [91] (+11)

2 8 5 11 8 [14] [11] [17] (+6, −3)

[3] 9 11 33 35 105 107 [321] (x3, +2)

Activity Page 89
50 5 100 10 200 <u>20</u> 400 40 <u>800</u> <u>80</u>
Rule: ÷10, x20

6 10 14 7 11 15 8 <u>12</u> <u>16</u> <u>9</u>
Rule: +4, +4, −7

987 876 765 654 <u>543</u> <u>432</u> <u>321</u>
Rule: Each digit is one less than the same digit in the previous number.

2 4 16 256 <u>65,536</u>
Rule: the number x itself
Original patterns will vary.

Chart 21
Used in conjunction with the activity page.

Activity Page 92

Chart 22
Used in conjunction with the activity page.

Activity Page 95

Rose Ecker   Roxanne Eaton

Essie Wood   [   ]   Esther Rich

Wilma Ross

Quilt pattern is Log Cabin.

Chart 23
Answers will vary, but should encompass the idea that Native Americans from different parts of North America hunted to provide food and clothing for their families. Hunting was an important part of traditional Native American culture.

Activity Page 98
Sentences should include the idea that what the Native Americans of different areas wore depended on the climate, availability of materials, and the amount of leisure time they had.

Chart 24
Answers will vary. For example: Wildflowers—More Than Just a Pretty Face; A Pharmacy in the Wilds

Activity Page 101
wintergreen—5; celandine—1; chamomile—3; eucalyptus—2; witch hazel—4

Chart 25
Used in conjunction with the activity page.

Activity Page 104

Frederick
Centennial High

Sophie
East Memorial
High

Allen
North High

Francesca
Uptown High

Critical Thinking

Chart 1
Used in conjunction with the activity page.

Activity Page 108
Groupings will vary but may include:
videos, printed material, sports equipment, broken, bird watching items, camping gear, baseball items

Chart 2
Used in conjunction with the activity page.

Activity Page 111
1. John Day
2. Crater Lake
3. Mt. Hood
4. north
5. northern
6. Lookout Mountain
7. Portland
8. Columbia River
9. Upper Klamath Lake
Bonus: It's on the bend of the river.

Chart 3
Smallest to largest by length: harbor seal, bottle-nosed dolphin, sea lion, manatee, elephant seal, humpback whale.

Animals may also be compared by weight.

Activity Page 114
Classifications will vary, but may include:
toothed/toothless, Pacific/Atlantic, warm water/cold water, ears/no ears, under 10 feet/over 10 feet, warm-blooded/cold-blooded, go on land/stay in water.

Chart 4
Desert: scorpions, sidewinders, coyotes, owls, deer, mice
Forest: moose, bobcats, weasels, skunks, black bears, owls, deer, mice
Grassland: bison, prairie dogs, pronghorn antelope, owls, deer, mice, coyotes
Desert/Forest: owls, deer, mice
Desert/Grassland: coyotes, owls, deer, mice
Forest/Grassland: owls, deer, mice
Desert/Forest/Grassland: owls, deer, mice

Activity Page 117
Answers will vary.

Chart 5

Students may have good reasons for classifying objects differently.

Activity Page 120

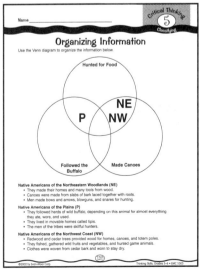

Chart 6

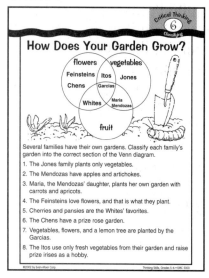

Activity Page 123

Answers will vary depending on the attributes chosen by the individual students. Pair students and have them evaluate each other's diagrams.

Chart 7

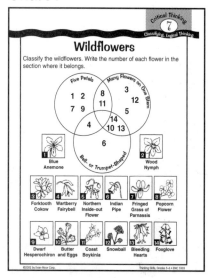

Activity Page 126

The pattern is a simple flower on a stem, multiple flowers on a stem.

Chart 8

Used in conjunction with the activity page.

Activity Page 129

5, 7, 12, 16

Chart 9

1. False—Alaska is part of the U.S. It is west of Canada.
2. False—The Andes Mountains are very high, and there isn't much oxygen to hold the heat at night. It can be very cold.
3. False—Russia is another neighbor.
4. False—The seasons are reversed in the Northern and Southern Hemispheres.
5. False—You travel southeast.
6. False—You travel northeast.
7. False—Much more land mass is located north of the equator, so it's reasonable to assume there is a greater population north of the equator.

Activity Page 132

Used in conjunction with the chart.

Chart 10

Answers will vary.

Activity Page 135

1. B; 2. A; 3. D; 4. E; 5. F; 6. C

Chart 11

Row 1—living/nonliving; Row 2—plants/ animals; Row 3—flowering plants/nonflowering plants; Row 4—daisy/living, plants, flowering plants

Activity Page 138

1. plant, flower, rose, tea rose
2. living thing, animal, insect, bumble bee
3. body part, head, eye, iris
4. body part, leg, foot, toes, nails
5. weather system, storm, tornado
6. dog
7. food or plant
8. Any of the following will do: snake, lizard, crocodile, turtle, dinosaur.
9. Answers will vary.